Advance Praise for *Fool Me Once*

"Rick Lax embedded himself with Vegas's most notorious magicians, call girls, and wheeler-dealers and emerged with a funny and fascinating cautionary tale for the rest of us. Anyone who's ever been scammed, bluffed, or lied to should read *Fool Me Once*."

—Kevin Roose, author of *The Unlikely Disciple: A Sinner's Semester at America's Holiest University*

"In a city where nothing is quite what it seems, Rick Lax introduces us to the showgirls, prostitutes, casino card counters, magicians, pickup artists, and street hustlers who work their short cons under the bright lights of the Las Vegas Strip. *Fool Me Once* is an illuminating read and terrific fun."   —David Grazian, author of *On the Make: The Hustle of Urban Nightlife*

"Plenty of cons and cheap hustles in this lively memoir of time spent on the seamier edge of Casinoland . . . An entertaining field guide to vice, but also one with a point—if you're headed anywhere near the Strip, watch your wallet."   —*Kirkus Reviews*

"Rick Lax has written a wry to the world of deception."   —Jim Steinmey

Praise for *Lawyer Boy*

"A hilarious memoir."   —*Las Vegas Review-Journal*

"First-time author Lax delivers an entertaining and sometimes zany look at the first year of law school. . . . Lax's discoveries of what he didn't expect offer fascinating up-to-date insights."   —*Publishers Weekly*

"I'll be buying his books for a long time to come."
        —A. J. Jacobs, author of *The Know-It-All* and *The Year of Living Biblically*

"A very entertaining work by a clever, hopeful, and unavoidably unscrupulous guy. My kinda book."
        —Harry Anderson, star of *Night Court* and *Dave's World*

"Rick Lax writes with a sharp wit and a fine sense of the absurd. *Lawyer Boy* might not help anyone succeed in law school, but it will certainly make the experience more enjoyable."
        —Steven Lubet, author of *Lawyers' Poker*

FOOL
ME
ONCE

ALSO BY RICK LAX

Lawyer Boy

FOOL ME ONCE

HUSTLERS,
HOOKERS,
HEADLINERS,
AND HOW
NOT TO GET
SCREWED
IN VEGAS

Rick Lax

ST. MARTIN'S GRIFFIN
NEW YORK

FOOL ME ONCE. Copyright © 2010 by Rick Lax. All rights reserved. Printed in the United States of America. For information, address St. Martin's Press, 175 Fifth Avenue, New York, N.Y. 10010.

Book design by Jonathan Bennett

Library of Congress Cataloging-in-Publication Data

Lax, Rick.
    Fool me once : hustlers, hookers, headliners, and how not to get screwed in Vegas / Rick Lax.—1st ed.
      p. cm.
    ISBN 978-0-312-54570-3
    1. Lax, Rick.—Anecdotes. 2. Las Vegas (Nev.)—Biography. 3. Las Vegas (Nev.)—Anecdotes. 4. Gambling—Nevada—Las Vegas—Anecdotes. 5. Casinos—Nevada—Las Vegas—Anecdotes. 6. Deception—Nevada—Las Vegas—Anecdotes. 7. Hoaxes—Nevada—Las Vegas—Anecdotes. 8. Swindlers and swindling—Nevada—Las Vegas—Anecdotes. I. Title.
F849.L35L395 2011
979.3'135—dc22

2010037869

First Edition: January 2011

10 9 8 7 6 5 4 3 2 1

Contents

1. An Earful of Cider 1

2. How I'd Gone from Studying for the Illinois Bar
   Exam to Cavorting with Las Vegas Prostitutes
   and Con Men in Such a Short Period of Time 15

3. Ridiculousness Is in the Eye of the Beholder 49

4. Rick Lax's 100 Percent Foolproof System for
   Sneaking into Nightclubs Without Paying
   Cover, Picking Up Beautiful Women in Under
   Forty-five Minutes, and Writing Overblown
   Chapter Titles 67

5. You Gotta Be Honestly Sincere 105

6. Control and the Illusion of It 131

7. The Hard Way to Make an Easy Twenty-three
   Hundred Dollars 149

8. Something You Can Do with a Hundred Dollars . . .171

9. Heroic Police Officer Prevents Disguised Idiot
   from Carrying Out Massive Terrorist Attack 197

10. Something George Clooney
     Might Do in a Clark Gable Biopic 231

11. The Rest of the Truth 259

     Epilogue: One Last Mindfreak 279

     CONTACTING THE AUTHOR 285

     AUTHOR'S NOTE 287

     ACKNOWLEDGMENTS AND PLUGS 291

1. An Earful of Cider

These women weren't dressed like your typical prostitutes. They were dressed like prostitutes who, for Halloween, had decided to go out as slutty hookers. You name the prostitute cliché and these two were on it like leopard print on a miniskirt. Fishnet stockings? Check. Thigh-high leather boots? Check. Sophia Loren eye shadow? Check.

They were sitting at a table for four and the other two seats were free, so I asked them whether my mom and I could join them for dinner.

"Of course, sweetie," the blond one said, mentally preparing herself for what was sure to be the weirdest request of her professional career.

We set our Panda Express trays down and my mom got the ball rolling:

"Where are you nice young ladies from?" she asked.

"We're both from Oakland, but we met on the Strip," the redhead said. "How about you?"

"Michigan, then Chicago," I told her.

"Yeah, you seem like a midwesterner," she replied.

"Well, be careful who you trust out here. Especially on the Strip. Everybody's working an angle."

She delivered the line with no apparent irony.

"What brought you to Vegas?" I asked the blonde.

"I needed a change. Needed to get away from some things. Plus I've always loved it here."

"I've got two kids," the redhead said. "Two-year-old and a five-year-old. This is where the business is, so this is where I am."

"And how is business?" I asked.

"Bad," she replied. "Economy—you know? Everybody's talking about 'bailout' this and 'bailout' that. All I know is I can't get a [slang term for a unit of currency] for a [slang term for a sex act]."

"That's terrible!" my mom said, leaving it unclear as to whether the terrible thing was the prostitute's vulgar language or the fact that the economy was so bad that she couldn't get a whichever for a whatever.

I told the hookers that I needed a change, too, that I loved Las Vegas, too, that I planned to spend a couple of weeks in the city, and that I planned to write about it.

The redhead said, "*I* should write a book. I've got more stories than everybody else in this city put together."

"Well, you have to tell me," I said. "Once my mom's gone, I mean. Give me your number so we can meet up sometime and you can, yeah, tell me about . . . your business."

"Sure, sweetie. So I can"—air quotes here—"*tell you about my business.*"

"Really," I said. "I mean, I'm not interested in *doing* business."

She shot me a look of offense.

"No . . . not . . . it's not that I don't think you're attractive. That's not . . . I just meant that I'm not in the *market*—"

"Not in the market . . . ?"

"I'm not *gay.* It's not *that.* I just want to *talk* about—"

"Here's my number."

The prostitutes excused themselves and walked out of the Palms Resort & Casino food court. I watched them make friends with some guy at the adjacent casino bar, and within a minute his arms were around their waists. Within two minutes, all three of them were throwing their heads back and laughing, looking as if they were being filmed for a Las Vegas Convention and Visitors Authority (LVCVA) TV spot.

The LVCVA is the group responsible for the "What happens here stays here" ad campaign, which centers around a handful of TV commercials promoting explicit lying.★ Most people know it as the "What happens in

★ One of these commercials features a guy approaching a dozen different women in a dozen locations on the Strip and telling each one of them that he has a different occupation. "I'm a rock star," `"I'm an astrophysicist"—that sort of thing. At the end of the commercial, the guy tells some woman that he's a writer and she replies, "You told my friend you were an attorney." He pauses, and then says, "I am . . . in the off-season." She doesn't believe him.

Nobody believes me when I tell them I'm a writer/lawyer, either.

Vegas stays in Vegas" campaign, but from a business point of view, the point is, *most people know it.*

When city advertising executives discuss what makes the "What happens" ads so successful, they say things like, "The beauty of the 'What happens' campaign is that it means different things to different people. It can mean everything from going to a risqué revue show to splurging on a fancy dinner." That characterization is as deceitful as the ad campaign itself; the "What happens" ad campaign's implication is crystal clear: *If you come to Las Vegas and gamble away your children's college fund and cheat on your wife with, say, two prostitutes you meet at the Palms food court, the city's tourism board will credit your bank account and fly you home in a time machine so you can un-cheat on your wife and preserve the sanctity of your marriage.* That message hits home with a lot of people; every year 40 million visit Las Vegas, and do their best to hang on to their money in the process.

Not all succeed—I saw that much firsthand, after I'd left the prostitutes and my mom back at the Palms.

Between Monte Carlo and New York New York, I came across a group of twenty or so tourists gathered in a tight cluster around a stack of milk crates. It was a three-card monte game. Now, two years ago, if you had told me you'd seen a real three-card monte game on Las Vegas Boulevard—not just a gambling demonstration performed by a magician—I'd have called you a liar. I'd have told you that three-card monte games exist only in outdated movies in which fast-talking men in bowler hats and high trousers recite antiquated poems that include phrases like "Hey Diddle Diddle" and "Hanky Poo."

The operator, a forty-something black guy wearing a Mighty Ducks jersey and Breitling watch—possibly a Brotling or a Breitline—was quick with his hands and with his words. He was friendly and funny. And I suppose he needed to be; he was taking everybody's money. Well, everybody except some white guy with long sideburns and a fraternity T-shirt.

Frat boy, I deduced, was a shill. He was working with the operator, and his job was to convince passersby that the game was winnable. The difference in age and race was no accident.

I stood behind the operator and watched the game for fifteen or twenty minutes. These guys were pros. At one point, the operator turned his back to the impromptu table he had constructed from two milk crates and a cardboard box top and asked me if I wanted to move to the front to get a better view. While he was saying this, an Asian lady wearing a Mandalay Bay T-shirt and Mandalay Bay baseball cap reached forward and bent up the upper-right corner of the "money card." The queen. The bend was slight but unmistakable. The operator turned back to the table, picked up the cards, but failed to notice the bend. He mixed the three cards and then asked for bets.

"Who's gonna bet? Someone's gonna bet. One bet to the highest bidder."

The Asian lady slapped a fifty in front of the center card, the one with the bend in its upper right-hand corner.

"Fifty dollars bet. Anybody want to bet more?"

Everybody wanted to bet more, including a dad who reached into his wallet and pulled out a stack of twenties.

"I got one forty on the middle card," he said, laying seven bills on the table.

"Sorry, lady," the operator said as he returned the Asian woman's fifty. "You know the rules: only one bet at a time, to the highest bidder."

She protested—in Japanese, I think—but to no avail.

"If you don't like it, take your money inside. They'll let you bet however much you want on whatever you want. Okay, we got one forty on the middle card. Any higher bets?"

I pulled out my wallet. I had more than three hundred dollars in it.

But I also had a piece of advice I'd picked up from my high school's production of *Guys and Dolls*. The advice comes from Sky Masterson and it was passed on to

Nathan Detroit, a gambler who wanted to bet Masterson that Mindy's restaurant sold more strudel than cheesecake:

> One of these days in your travels, a guy is going to show you a brand-new deck of cards on which the seal is not yet broken. This man is going to offer to bet you that he can make the jack of spades jump out of the deck and squirt cider in your ear. Now son, do not bet this man, for sure as you stand there, you're going to wind up with an earful of cider.

The moral is that if a bet seems too good to be true, it probably is. I knew this advice, yet I was still very tempted to bet. I had the money, I had the edge, and I knew exactly where the queen was.

It was on the left, not in the middle.

You see, I knew that the Asian tourist in the Mandalay Bay shirt and hat wasn't really a tourist; she was another shill. I knew that the bent corner was part of the act, that the operator had removed the bend from the queen with his right pinky and that he put another one in the four of clubs by pressing it against the table.

"Any more bets? Any more bets?"

I stuck my pinky in my ear to check for cider and then returned my money to my pocket. The operator turned over the center card and showed that it was the four of clubs. The queen was on the left. I'd been right.

Still, I probably made the right choice in not betting. Even if I did throw my cash next to the queen, it's unlikely I would have walked away three hundred dollars richer. The operator probably would have picked up the two of clubs, the card that hadn't been bent at any point, and used it to execute a *Mexican turnover,* a move in which you use one card to turn over a second and switch the two in the process. And what would I have said in response? "That's a *Mexican turnover*"? Oh, I'm sure *that* would have persuaded him. If I had thrown my money down and turned over the card myself, he would have said that I'd broken the rules of the game by touching the cards, and that the violation invalidated my bet.

The operator scooped up the midwestern dad's twenties and resumed the game . . . until he got the signal that the cops were coming. The signal didn't come from either of the men I'd pegged as lookouts. It came from one of the guys who populate the Strip handing out advertisements for escort services.* The operator slipped the cards in his pocket, tossed the box top in a nearby trash can, and kicked the milk carts toward the street.

The Asian tourist walked north toward Monte Carlo;

---

* According to the *Las Vegas Review-Journal,* these men and women, many of whom are illegal immigrants, make $4.50 per hour and face jail time if they accidentally block a sidewalk or a trash can.

the operator walked south toward New York New York; frat guy pulled out his cell phone and started a conversation with his imaginary stockbroker. I tapped him on the shoulder and said, "Looks like today's your lucky day."

Terrible opening line. I sounded just like a cop.

"Guess so," he said, and then he returned to his imaginary call.

"Well, I'm sorry to interrupt your call"—I paused and looked at him in a way that was meant to convey that I knew the call was fake (if I were a cop, I'd know how to execute this look perfectly)—"but I wanted to talk to you about the game."

"I'm telling you, you can beat that game if you watch the guy carefully."

It was a stock line. He'd been saying it again and again like a broken record player for the past twenty minutes.

"I *was* watching carefully. I'm a magician. That's why I want to talk with you about your game. So how long have you been out here?"

"Fifteen minutes."

He folded up his phone and returned it to his pocket (without even saying good-bye).

"No, I mean, *how long have you been out here?*"

"If you're being serious about the magic thing," he told me, "then let me give you some advice:"—*bet it doesn't involve cider*—"Go away."

The real cop wore a yellow shirt and had a belt with two walkie-talkies. He might have been a casino security guard, come to think of it. But either way, he didn't look twice at the cardboard box top in the trash can or the milk crates near the street. He was just passing by, not prowling for monte games.

"Where you from?" I asked the shill.

"Where are *you* from?" he replied.

"Michigan, then Chicago."

"Where in Chicago?" he asked.

"Downtown."

"I'm from the Southside."

The shill looked around, presumably to see whether any of his partners were in sight.

"I've been doing this for a couple months," he told me. "On and off."

Apparently the Chicago connection did the trick.*

---

* In 2004, a group of Santa Clara University psychologists discovered that people are nicer to people with whom they share an arbitrary connection. Research subjects were asked to complete a meaningless questionnaire that included basic personal information such as birthday. A confederate—that's the academic term for shill—seated next to the real subject snuck a peek at the subject's form and memorized her birthday. The psychologist administering the bogus study collected the forms and then asked the subject and confederate for their birthdays, always querying the confederate first. In the control group, the confederate gave her actual birthday. In the experimental group, the confederate claimed to have the same birthday as the subject. After filling out bogus personality tests, the subject and confederate were told that the study was over and that they could leave the room. That's when the real study began. On the way out, the confederate asked the subject whether she would read an eight-page essay he had written for class and write a one-page summary on the persuasiveness of his arguments. Thirty-four percent of the subjects from the control group agreed, compared with 62 percent of the subjects from the experimental group.

"I owned a construction company back in Chicago. I employed five to ten guys, depending on the season, on the job. Then the economy turned around and there were no construction jobs. So, I came to Vegas to look for work, but there was none here either, turned out."

For a while everybody thought Las Vegas was immune to the recession. But when Boyd Gaming Corporation abandoned its plans to build the five-thousand-room mega-resort known as Echelon (after spending $500 million on concrete and steel), people weren't so sure. And a couple months later, after Las Vegas Sands Corporation nixed its $600 million condominium project, locals got the message: The recession had hit Vegas, too.

"So the other guys are other out-of-work construction workers?" I asked.

"No, just met them here, randomly."

"Good gig?"

"That's a stupid question. And you know it's a stupid question. This is a shit gig. Just a matter of time before we get busted. Some of these guys *have* been busted before. But yeah, it'd be a great gig if I could do it forever without getting caught. Only thing that stops people from taking other people's money is the fear of getting caught. I'm going back to Chicago as soon as I get the chance."

"Me, too," I lied. As I told the hookers, I love Las Vegas.

Now, I'm no psychologist—this according to my undergraduate psychology professors—but my love of Las

Vegas probably also has something to do with my first experiences in the city. My dad was one of the first people to read Edward Thorp's *Beat the Dealer,* and was quick to teach himself how to count cards. He took my mom and me to Las Vegas every year. Caesars Palace put us up in big suites, comped our meals, and gave us tickets to see Siegfried & Roy and Lance Burton.

Back on the Strip, the three-card monte operator returned and restacked his milk crates.

"Back to work," the shill said. "And just so you know, I'm the friendly one. These other guys aren't going to talk to you. Or, if they do, if they're friendly, it's 'cause

I'm not saying my parents were overprotective; I'm just saying they apparently brought a child safety seat out to the Caesars Palace pool.

they want something from you. And you don't want that. You saw our show. You saw our moves. So if I were you, I'd probably head somewhere else at this point."

At that point, I headed elsewhere, and as I did, I wondered how I'd gone from studying for the Illinois Bar Exam to cavorting with Las Vegas prostitutes and con men in such a short period of time.

Well, let me tell you how. . . .

2. How I'd Gone from Studying for the Illinois Bar Exam to Cavorting with Las Vegas Prostitutes and Con Men in Such a Short Period of Time

All my friends had backstage passes to Kanye West's 2008 Lollapalooza performance and I didn't. But I wasn't upset. I wasn't even familiar with West's music. I knew he'd won a handful of Grammys for his album *The College Dropout,* that he wears Shutter Shades, and that he said, "George Bush doesn't care about black people" on live television, but that was it.

The "passes" were actually neon green wristbands with a picture of the Chicago skyline on one side and "Kanye West" written on the other. My friends had gotten them because their band, Tally Hall, had played at the festival earlier that day. I'd received a pass to their performance, but that was it.

Aside from Tally Hall, Kanye West, and Radiohead, I wasn't familiar with any of the Lollapalooza artists, and I wasn't in the mood to fight my way through the sweaty, pulsating masses just to discover a new band, use a non-flushing plastic toilet, or buy a cup of warm beer. I prefer to take in my music with air-conditioning, porcelain toilettes, and a cold martini. So after Tally Hall finished its set, I left the festival and met up with my friend Marty, a fellow law student graduate and fellow magician.

"You have to sneak backstage," he told me.

"Since when are you a Kanye West fan?" I asked.

"No, you have to do it for the sake of doing it. And so you can tell people you did."

"I'd rather be backstage at a Moxy Früvous concert."

"Who's that?" Marty asked.

"Exactly," I said.

"What I'm taking from this conversation is that you don't think you can do it."

"I could if I wanted to."

"I doubt it."

Well, that settled that.

I walked to CVS and bought a Sharpie, a roll of paper towels, and a bottle of fantastik. My plan was to remove "Tally Hall" from the wristband and replace it with "Kanye West." I returned to my apartment, sprayed some fantastik onto a sheet of paper towel, and rubbed away. To no avail. The Sharpie wouldn't come off . . . which is probably why the security guard had used a Sharpie in the first place.

Next I sprayed the fantastik directly onto the wristband

and let it sit there for a couple of minutes. When I wiped the spray off, all of "Hall" and most of "Tally" came with it . . . along with a significant chunk of the printed building design. So at that point, I not only had to add "West" and somehow change what was left of "Tally" into "Kanye," but I also had to redraw the Chicago skyline.

The reconstructed buildings looked like Frank Gehrys. The original buildings were matted onto the wristband; my hand-drawn replacements reflected even the weakest of lights. And then there was the whole "Tally"/"Kanye" discrepancy—I wasn't about to spray any more fantastik on the wristband to remedy it. The *a* and the *y* were fine—they worked for both "Kanye" and "Tally"—and adding an *e* would be no problem at all. The trouble was turning the *T* into a *K* and the *ll* into an *n*.

So here's what I did:

I transformed the *T* into a monstrous, deformed *K*— the kind of a *K* a kindergartener would get smacked for drawing—by doubling its height and adding a diagonal appendage, which, like its first appendage (originally the cross of the *T*), protruded from both sides. I connected the top of the first *l* to the bottom of the second to create an uppercase *N*.

The second letter was now lowercase and the third letter was now uppercase, and to keep the pattern going, I had to add an uppercase *E* and then write "wEsT" in a similarly case-alternating fashion. In the end, my wristband looked like a teenage girl's social-networking profile.* So, assuming the security guard checking wristbands had poor eyesight, no flashlight, and confused my wristband with his daughter's MySpace page, I had nothing to worry about.

Three hours later, I returned to Grant Park and approached the guard who would decide my evening's fate. He stood before an opening in the chain-link fence that separated Chicago's musical proletariats from its musical bourgeoisie. Most people in my situation would have flashed the doctored wristband quickly, but that, I realized, would have only invited a second, more careful inspection. I went the opposite route and made a big show of pushing my sleeve back and holding my wrist about twelve inches away from the guard's shaved head, as if I had nothing to hide. If anything, the wristband was too close for him to get a clear look at it . . . and too close for him to shine a flashlight on.

As I held my arm up, I said, "You know if the show's going to finish up before or after they end the whole festival or what?"

The question made no sense, and that was the point.

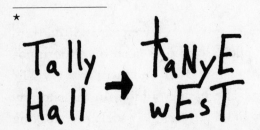

I wanted the guard spending his brain cells deciphering my question's meaning, as opposed to scrutinizing my wristband.

So, did my plan work?

Did my wristband fool the guard?

You bet it didn't.

"That's not a Kanye band. You changed it up."

It took him like half a second.

"It's all shiny and shit," he continued. "You drew this with marker. What, you just had a pass to some other group and changed it up?"

"Actually, yes," I admitted. "That's exactly what I did."

"Good try, but no."

I smiled, shook the guard's hand, and said, "When I become a rock star, I want you working the door."

He laughed and asked, "You a big Kanye fan or what?"

I once read in a fortune cookie that whenever one door closes, another one opens. Or maybe I read that in a Tony Robbins book or heard it on an episode of *Step by Step*. But the point is, another door opened.

"*College Dropout* is pretty much my all-time favorite album," I said. "But it's not just Kanye's music, you know; it's who he is. His beliefs. Like when he was talking about George Bush, I was like, *Yeah, right on, Kanye!*"★

★ For the record, I don't actually believe our former president "doesn't care about black people."

19

"Ha! I saw that, too. I was like, *Right on, brotha!*"

"Oh, for sure."

"Tell you what," the guard said. "If you like Kanye so much, get in there. Just don't show your wristband to the other guys. Keep your sleeve rolled down. Got it?"

"I got it."

I shook the guard's hand again and walked through the opening. As I did, the guard said, "I'm letting you in because you were straight with me and owned up to what you did. Most guys would just run away or deny it."

"No kidding," I replied. "There's so many dishonest people out there."

Backstage, I drank my fair share of Southern Comfort, chatted up a couple of music journalists, and pretended to know the musicians they were talking about. West arrived via bus a minute before he went onstage, and he left as soon as he was done. The real excitement came at the Hard Rock Hotel afterparty. I got past the clipboard girl and bouncer out front by telling them I was Tally Hall's manager.★ They let my then-girlfriend, Elena, in, too, no questions asked.

No surprise there. That's how it usually worked for Elena, but more on that later.

The afterparty had everything: beautiful people, top-shelf liquor, live entertainment, a team of tattoo artists,

---

★ And I was. For like two months. A couple years back.

and a LifeStyles photo booth that dispensed condoms along with photos. I got in the booth with a communications major who once posed for *Playboy*,[*] and a girl who, when I asked her what she did, looked around the room and said, "This, mostly."

The Bunny and pro partier escorted me (but not Elena—sorry, baby!) into the VIP area, where we sat in beanbag chairs, ate gourmet hot dogs and Dippin' Dots, banged a gong,[†] and chatted with the cast of this TV show that I really like but you haven't heard of.[‡] Supposedly, Lindsay Lohan had left the room just before we walked in. Spent the whole time sending text messages, we were told. I befriended some bass player with greasy hair and a tux jacket, and before he left he gave me a rolled-up pink wristband.

"It's an artist pass," he told me. "Unroll it, put it on, walk into that room there, and ask for a backpack."

He pointed across the hall to a room with a closed door that had a sign that read: *ARTISTS ONLY*. Luckily for me, I've always considered myself an artist of life (my city is my canvas, my soul is my paintbrush . . . you get the idea), so I reattached the wristband, opened the door, and walked inside. Ten or fifteen backpacks lay on the ground next to a girl wearing all sorts of official-looking badges and tags.

---

[*] According to her, not my subsequent Google search.
[†] This is not a euphemism; there was a gong at the party.
[‡] *Human Giant*—see?

"Can I get a backpack?"

"Artist?" she asked.

"Tally Hall."

"Didn't you guys get gifted a half hour ago?"

"*I* didn't."

Technically true.

She handed me a hiking backpack, which, I later discovered, contained a Snowflake USB microphone, a pair of green and yellow Skullcandy headphones, a bottle of Diesel cologne, a Hard Rock T-shirt, several Rock the Vote thongs, a couple bottles of Fuze fruit drink, and a couple more LifeStyles condoms. The woman asked me my waist size and tossed me a pair of designer jeans that probably cost more than all my other jeans combined.

I walked out of the room and into Elena. She was waiting for me in the hallway, tapping her foot like a sitcom wife.

"So you're an *artist* now?" she wanted to know. She must have seen the sign.

"Of sorts," I replied.

"Lying doesn't count as art, you know."

"Depends on who's doing the lying."

Probably the coolest thing I'd ever said.

I'd met Elena when I first moved to Chicago in 2005, back when she was working at the International Latino Cultural Center and dating an amateur boxer. (She's five-three; he was six-four.) We fell out of contact in 2006, and then she e-mailed me out of the blue in the spring of

2008. She was single, I was single, and neither of us had much free time. The quintessential urban fairy tale.

"Hang on," said Elena, digging through her purse to find her ringing cell phone. "I think this is Arthur."

Okay, we *would* have been the quintessential urban fairy tale if it weren't for Arthur Soto. He wasn't "the other man"; he was Elena's boss.

Sort of.

She hung up the phone and said, "He needs my help."

"With what?"

"Research."

"Sunday night? At one in the morning?"

"He said 'research.'"

"It's not even like you have any experience doing legal research," I said.

"I told you, I do it on Google."

"Yeah, that's not legal research. You do legal research on Westlaw or Lexis."

"Arthur does that stuff. I do the auxiliary."

Elena had first mentioned Arthur three weeks earlier. She told me that she'd met him on MySpace. *Sketchy.* She told me that he offered her a paralegal position before even meeting her in person. *Very sketchy.* She told me that he hadn't even asked to see her résumé, which was convenient for Elena because she didn't have one.

Oh, and she told me Arthur was going to pay her ninety-five thousand dollars a year.

Incredibly fucking sketchy.

I Googled Arthur's name and found a sparse LinkedIn profile, a stale blog, and an elaborate MySpace profile filled with pictures of conference rooms, corner offices, and nothing else. Most of Arthur's Top 8 friends were in bikinis. I assumed he offered Elena the job because he wanted to sleep with her, simple as that. And as time went by and as Elena told me more and more about this "job" Arthur had given her, I began to suspect something more was going on.

"Where's his office, again?" I asked.

"The Loop."

"Where in the Loop?"

"I forget the exact streets, if that's what you're asking."

"So how do you plan to get there? How *have* you been getting there?"

"I told you I do the research in my building's computer center."

"So he just wants you at a computer right now?" I asked.

"Right."

"But you have been to his office before. . . ."

"Yes."

"Does he have partners?"

"I don't know."

"How many people did you see when you went there?"

"I didn't go in."

"You didn't go *inside?*"

"Right."

"Have you *ever* been inside the building?"

"We met outside the building that one afternoon when he took me to lunch. I thought I told you that last week."

"You did, but you didn't tell me that was the only time you'd been to his office. I assumed you'd been going in all these days."

Elena shrugged.

"So you're really going to leave the party?" I said. "We didn't even get our complimentary tattoos. I thought we could get each other's names tattooed on our foreheads."

"Tempting, but no. I have to go. Especially tonight— I mean, he's giving me his car to drive to Ohio tomorrow, so I don't want to piss him off tonight."

"I just can't believe you're doing so much work for this guy and you haven't even seen a paycheck yet."

"He said I'd get the first one in two more weeks. I think that's standard for the first check. But anyway, I don't want to upset him 'cause I have no other way of getting there."

"And what's in Ohio, again?"

"My friend's gallery is reopening. I told you all this."

"Oh, right, Sofia. The flamingo girl."

"She paints other things," Elena said.

"I didn't mean that as an insult. I like her flamingo stuff."

"Stop."

"I'm serious. Your friend is to flamingos as Monet is to hay—"

Elena's cell rang again. She picked it up.

"Okay . . . okay, I can. . . . Twenty minutes. . . . I . . . okay . . . okay. Bye."

Elena hung up the phone and said, "I've got to leave now. I'm sorry. I'll stop by your place tomorrow morning, before I head out. What time will you be up?"

"Ten."

"See you at ten."

She kissed me and started to walk away.

"This . . . ," I started to say.

Elena turned around.

"Something about this," I said, "is off. Something about this guy. You *must* sense that."

"Are you sure you're not just upset I'm leaving the party?"

"I mean, I am, but that's separate."

"It's fine. Don't be so paranoid," Elena said.

"I'm not being paranoid."

"I'll be fine."

Elena was way off on that one.

I lived on the thirty-second floor of the Frontier Plaza building in downtown Chicago. No matter how far I go in life, no matter how much I make and how much I succeed, I'll never again live in such a cool apartment. Problem was, every year the building's management hiked up my rent around $150 per month. My lease was coming to an end at the end of July and I had no plans to renew.

Elena knocked on my door at 11:00 A.M. She was an hour late and I'd overslept. I was supposed to meet Marty for lunch at noon, and I still needed to shower and catch the train.

"I told Arthur to send the car here at twelve," she said. "I hope that's okay."

"It's fine, but how is he sending a car over?"

"He said he's having two of his guys come in separate cars and then drive back in one."

"So he has two assistants in addition to you?"

"Apparently."

"And now he has them both working for you?"

"That's what he said. He said he's going to call me when they're five minutes away."

"And that doesn't seem odd to you?"

"Don't you have to shower?"

I showered, changed, wished Elena a safe drive, and took the Brown Line north to Belmont. Marty and I met up for burgers at Clarke's on Belmont, and then we played some Ping-Pong. When I returned home at 4:00 P.M., Elena was still there.

"You're still here."

"I'm still here."

She hadn't moved from the futon.

"What happened to the ride?" I asked.

"Something with one of the tires. Arthur had the guys take it in for a change, and I guess they found something else wrong with the car—something with the transmission—so now they're fixing that. But that's supposed to be done any minute now, and then they're coming right over. I just need them to get here fast because I told Sofia I'd be at the gallery an hour before everything started."

"I wish I could stay here and wait with you, but I'm supposed to go to Barnes and Noble by school—"

"Don't worry about me. Just go. I'll be fine."

I went, and I came back around 8:00 P.M. Elena was still there, still on the futon, still hadn't moved an inch.

"Traffic," she said. "They're caught in traffic now. I don't even know if I'll make it before it's over."

"How much traffic could there be?"

"A lot?"

"Have you eaten?"

"A little."

"What'd you have?"

"Some stuff out of your fridge."

I checked the fridge but couldn't find anything missing.

"So where are the cars now?" I asked.

"A half hour ago he told me Lincoln Park. And I called three or four times a couple minutes ago, and it kept going to voice mail. Rang once or twice, then voice mail."

"You mean, sometimes once, sometimes twice?"

"Yeah. . . ."

"Elena, he's screening your calls and then sending them to voice mail. Let's try calling him from my phone."

"No!"

I'd never heard Elena object so vociferously to anything.

"Why can't I call him?" I asked.

"Because you don't need to. And I don't want to upset him. Everything is going to be fine."

I suspect that at that point Elena was no longer trying to convince me; she was trying to convince herself.

"What's his number?"

She handed me her cell. I found Arthur's number and dialed it on my own phone. When it started ringing, I handed it over to Elena.

"Hi, Arthur, it's El—Yeah, from Rick's phone. I'm in his apartment, waiting for . . . Okay. . . . Okay, but the drive is really long, and I need time to . . . Yeah, but it's . . . No, that's fine, as long as they . . . Yeah, as long as they can make it by ten, I still want . . . I still want the car, yes. . . . Okay, thanks."

She hung up.

"What the hell?" I said. "Why didn't you tell him your calls were going to voice mail?"

"I didn't want to *confront* him," Elena replied. "He's doing me a big favor here!"

"He's *not,* though. Where's the favor?! Where's the car?!"

"It's coming! They stopped at Burger King."

"And he knows that because . . . apparently *their* calls are getting through to him. And so are mine. Just not yours. And you don't find that suspicious? I'll bet if we called him from my phone again he wouldn't pick up."

"Don't!"

"What are you so afraid of?"

"I told you, I don't want to cause any—"

I called again. To voice mail after one ring.

Elena and I waited in silence for the next twenty minutes. At 8:30, I said, "If the car doesn't show up by nine, will you—"

"They're going to be here in a minute."

"But *if* they're not, if they don't show up by nine—*nine hours after the time they were supposed to arrive*—will you be ready to . . . ?"

"To . . . ?"

"To accept that this whole thing—"

Elena's phone rang. It was Arthur, saying that the car had arrived.

Well, I'll be.

We took the elevator down and walked outside to the pickup area.

But there were no cars waiting.

"Maybe they're out front," Elena suggested.

We walked to the front. No cars there, either.

"Call him back," I said.

She did and he picked up.

"They're not here," Elena told him. "They're . . . No, they're not; we're standing outside right now, and we don't see . . . We *did* circle around."

She hung up.

"He said he's going to call them and call me back. Maybe they're at the wrong building."

Five minutes passed by. Then ten minutes. Elena tried calling him back, but it went to voice mail. She left a message asking where the cars were and whether she could have the phone number of one of the drivers. Arthur called her back and Elena put it on speaker.

"They've been waiting there for fifteen minutes," Arthur said. "I don't know what to tell you. Frontier Plaza. They're *there*."

"They *aren't* here!" Elena said. "We're downstairs and there are no cars here."

"They're there," Arthur said. "What's wrong with you? They've called me three times, asking where you are."

"There aren't any cars here! Are you sure they're at *Frontier Plaza* on *Michigan Avenue*?"

"I'm sure," said Arthur, "and honestly, I can't believe you're using that tone with me right now. I'm trying to do you a huge favor, and you're being incredibly disrespectful."

Elena wasn't using any "tone."

"Hang on," Arthur said. "I'm getting another call."

He hung up.

"Elena," I said, "you have to listen to me now. This guy is fucking with you. I don't know why, but he is. There are no cars. There are no assistants. There is no job. Whatever . . . *research* you've been doing for this guy— whatever you want to call it—it's not what a paralegal does. A paralegal goes into an office every day, and—"

"But why would he—why would *anyone* . . . string me along like this?"

"I have no idea, but I do know that if this guy was really trying to get you a car so you could go to your friend's gallery, he'd have been more concerned with logistics and less concerned with 'respect' and with your 'tone.'"

When we got back up to my room, she pounded on the futon and pounded on her knees. Good signs, I thought. The truth was finally hitting her.

"Are you hungry?" I asked.

"No."

"Can we get some food?"

"I'm not hungry," she said.

"I know you're not, but I am"—not true—"so let's go get burritos."

"You know what I really need?"

"What?"

"Some wine."

"You haven't eaten all day," I said.

32

"But I'm not hungry."

"You are. You're just anxious right now."

"Can I please just have some of the zin on the counter?"

I poured her half a glass.

"I can't have a full glass?"

"After you eat a burrito you can have a full glass."

We walked to Qdoba on Randolph. Neither of us said anything. Elena ordered a vegetarian burrito, but she didn't eat much of it. Every bite was a chore, every swallow a pain. She complained of bad taste, dry mouth, and upset stomach.

"Do you have any tequila at your place?" she wanted to know.

"Finish the burrito; then we'll talk alcohol."

"No offense, Ricky, but I know what I need better than you. And what I need is to relax. I'll be okay. I just need to relax, have some drinks. Maybe go out, even."

"We can go out if you want; I just don't think drinking right now is the best idea."

"Let me put it like this: I'm going to head home, get changed, and then I'm going to go out drinking. I'd really like it if you came with me, but if you don't want to, I'm still going to go."

"Fine. I'll come."

I met Elena at some dive bar in Wicker Park I'd been to once before. I picked the place thinking Elena would hate it and want to go home early. I was wrong; she apparently knew the fifty-something bartender, and before I'd arrived he'd hooked her up with a couple glasses of absinthe. She told me that *after* I'd bought her two glasses of merlot and one shot of Sambuca, mind you.

On the way out, Elena suggested we "take a little nap" on the sidewalk.

"Let's take a nap in a cab instead," I said, but by the time I finished saying it she'd plopped down on the sidewalk.

One doesn't appreciate how short a dress is until the girl who's wearing it is horizontal on pavement. I removed my vest and covered Elena the best I could, but still a small crowd started to form. A guy in cowboy boots asked if I wanted his help hailing a cab, and I said yes.

It wasn't Elena's vomit that upset the cabdriver. What upset the cabdriver was that she waited until the very last second of the ride to spew. We had already stopped in my apartment's driveway. She had only to open the door, lean over, and release. The bulk of the vomit went on her lap, but a lot of it poured onto the cab's seat and floor, too.

I handed the driver all the cash I had on me, but I doubt it was enough to cover the cleanup cost. I walked around and picked up Elena using the bear hug technique, pressing pieces of vomited burrito between us. I persuaded the front-desk security guard to help me get

Elena's limp body onto one of the lobby's benches. We did everything we could to wake her. Sprinkled her face with water. Shouted. Slapped her. No response.

I told the guard to call 911, and she did. When the ambulance arrived, I told the medic everything I knew. He said he'd drive Elena to the hospital and pump her stomach. He said that everything was going to be fine.

Then Elena went missing. The hospital told me they'd discharged her early in the morning, but her roommate told me she'd never come home.

She was nowhere to be found. I contacted Elena's friends and her sisters through Facebook because I didn't have their phone numbers or e-mail addresses. Nobody had heard from her. I still had Arthur's phone number stored in my phone (from when we called to ask about the car), so I dialed it.

"Arthur Soto."

"Hi, Arthur. My name is Rick, and I'm trying to find Elena."

"Rick *Lax*?"

He knows my last name? That can't be good.

"Yes. . . ."

"Don't worry so much about Elena. She's not with me right now. But you shouldn't get so worked up about her. From the way she talks about you, it sounds like you can be a bit overprotective, and I'll tell you this about women: They don't like it when a guy—"

35

I hung up and took a cab to the police station to file a missing-person report.

"How long has she been gone?" the officer behind the counter asked.

"How do you know it's a she?"

"Is it a she?" he asked.

"Yes."

"So how long has she been gone?"

"A day."

"I'll take down the information, but there's not much we can do at this point."

"There are extenuating circumstances."

"Like what?"

I told the officer everything that had happened. I told him about Arthur, about the alcohol, and about the hospital trip.

"Okay, I've got everything down, but like I said, there's not much we can do at this point. Keep me updated if anything happens or if she shows up."

I didn't recognize the phone number, but it wasn't Arthur's, so I picked up.

"Is this Rick Lax?" The voice on the other end was lower and had a slight accent.

"Who is this?" I said.

"Detective Mike Jhadav. I'm with the CPD."

"How do I know that?"

"Did you file a missing-person report with Officer Brummel earlier today? Big guy at the desk?"

"Yes."

"For Elena Ortiz?"

"Yes."

"Okay then. Officer Brummel gave me the report."

"Okay."

"I'm calling because I think your friend Elena could be in danger. The guy you mentioned in the report, Arthur Soto . . ."

"Yes . . ."

"Well, first of all, Arthur Soto is an alias; his real name is Arthur Solano. He's not a lawyer or a stockbroker or a real estate guy or whatever he told your friend he was."

"Lawyer."

"Right, he's not that. He's a drug dealer."

"Okay."

"And he's done this before, with other women."

"Done?"

"Auditioned them—whatever you want to call it. Interviewed them, strung them along for weeks—one time five months. Let me ask you: Do you know if he met her over the Internet?"

"That's what Elena said."

"And my daughter wants to know why I won't let her have a MySpace account. . . . Anyway, I say that your friend could be in danger because this Solano guy has a history of assault. He's been to jail for assault a couple of times. Serious assault, as in he shot people. Not girls, these were other dealers—guys who were trying to break up deals of his. But still, I'm concerned about your friend. Do you have a recent photo of her that you could e-mail me?"

"I can send you the link to her MySpace profile. There's lots of pictures on there."

"No, just e-mail me the actual photos. We can't access MySpace from the station."

"I can send you photos—sure. What else?"

"The big question is, is she with Solano right now?"

"I talked with Solano right before I came down. He said she wasn't with him, but I'm not sure if that makes it less or more likely that she is. I could give you his number—"

"Oh, I've got his number. I've got all his info."

"Maybe I'm missing something here," I said, "but if this guy is so bad and if you know all about him and have his information, why isn't he in jail?"

"He got out."

"He escaped?"

"No, he got out. He was released."

"Why?"

"How much do you know about the law?" Detective Jhadav asked.

"A lot, actually. I'm studying for the Bar Exam."

"Let me rephrase my question: How much do you know about how the law really works?"

"Maybe you better just say what you're getting at," I said.

"Until this guy kills somebody, he's going to be on the street doing this stuff."

Elena knocked on my door around 9:00 P.M. She was wearing the same short dress she'd been wearing two nights earlier, but it looked like it had been washed.

"*Now* I'm hungry," she said.

"Where were you?"

"Couple of places."

"Just tell me, were you with him?"

"I wasn't with him."

"You swear?"

"Yes."

I called the CPD and told them to call off the search. I fed Elena two Kashi waffles, two kiwis, and one and a half Balance protein bars. I told her what the detective had told me about Arthur. She didn't seem all that surprised or concerned . . . and that surprised and concerned me. Had she known more about Arthur than she'd let on? Had there been something more going on between them?

An hour later, Elena and I decided that maybe we weren't right for each other.

"If you still want to work as a paralegal," I said, "I can help you try to find a job."

"You don't have to do that. I'll find something. I'll be fine."

I didn't believe her, but I also didn't believe her well-being was my responsibility any longer.

Solano called me a few days later.

"Rick, it's Arthur—Elena's boss."

Fuck.

He must have stored my number from when I called him looking for Elena.

"Look," he began. "I'm calling to tell you I'm sorry. I was rude to you on the phone the other day, and there's no excuse for that."

I said nothing.

"I'm also calling because I'm looking for Elena. Guess the tables have turned!"

He said it like he was expecting a laugh.

"I'm thinking this is a pattern with her," Solano said. "Anyway, she hasn't been at work for a couple days now, and she's not picking up her phone, and I'm starting to get worried. Any idea where she is?"

"Find some other girl to fuck with. And don't contact me again."

"Did you tell her not to contact me?"

I hung up, and he called me right back.

I didn't pick up.

So he called again, and again.

"What were you thinking?!"

I probably shouldn't have told my mom anything.

"I'll tell you what you were thinking," she continued. "You weren't thinking!"

"Please calm down."

"You've got a murderer calling you on the phone and you want me to calm down?!"

"He's not a murderer. He didn't *kill* anybody. He just shot some people. *Not fatally*. And that's only because they interfered with his drug deals."

"Oh, that's reassuring. Promise me you won't see this Elena girl again."

"We broke up."

"And promise me you'll change your phone number."

"If this guy wants to get to me, he can get to me regardless of my phone number."

"Ricky!"

Probably shouldn't have said that, either.

"And promise me you'll at least get out of Chicago for a while, until this all blows over."

"I promise."

I'd already been planning on getting out of Chicago after the Bar Exam for a couple weeks. I wanted to clear my head before beginning the job hunt. Most of my classmates had started searching for jobs at the start of the school year, but I wasn't as concerned about finding a job as they were because the kind of job I wanted wasn't that sought after. I wanted to work at a personal injury firm. I wanted to be in the courtroom yelling at people, but I didn't want to deal with criminals or divorcing families every day. So by process of elimination, that left personal injury.

Now, a lot of soon-to-be lawyers go backpacking through Europe after they take the Bar Exam. The idea is, as an attorney, you won't have any free time until retirement, so you might as well have some fun while you have the chance. The first flaw in that theory is that backpacking isn't fun. Backpacking is miserable. Maybe backpacking was fun when backpacks were first invented and the alternative was hiking around carrying your stuff on a platter, but today backpacks should be reserved for elementary-school children and twenty-somethings posing as musicians to get free Rock the Vote thongs.

I admit that it took me a while to figure that out, how awful backpacking is. When I was a kid, I constantly bugged my dad, a tax attorney, to take me hiking. "I don't spend all day at the office so I can sleep in a plastic shack filled with mosquitoes," he'd say. So for years I thought my dad a bore and imagined how much fun he and I would have in the middle of the woods, telling ghost stories, eating s'mores, and doing all the other things father-and-son hiking teams did on television.

Then I actually went backpacking, through Michigan's Porcupine Mountains, with ten other boys from Camp Nebagamon. For one week, I carried my clothing, my sleeping bag, my sleeping mat,★ and a tent across murky streams and muddy mountain paths. No distractions, no interruptions, no artificiality. Just me, my peers, my counselor, and Mother Nature.

Easily the worst seven days of my entire life. It gave me a newfound respect for my father's judgment.

The second flaw in that theory is that if backpacking through Europe is your idea of fun, you probably shouldn't become a lawyer. Nothing is more dissimilar from hiking through the Old World than researching the Federal Rules of Civil Procedure in a New York high-rise office building. I'd liken an attorney's post-bar European backpack excursion to a traditional bachelor party in that if your idea of fun is getting plastered with the guys and getting lap dances from strippers, then you probably shouldn't be getting married.

Or maybe you should be marrying the stripper.

I like being indoors. Air-conditioning and porcelain toilets are just the icing on the cake that is Tyvek insulation, instant-hot faucets, and high-definition television.

★ The sleeping mat was like a yoga mat, only thinner. The other boys didn't have mats, and they referred to mine as a "wussy mat."

My favorite rain forest is the fake one in the middle of The Mirage.* My favorite sunset is the one at the Caesars Forum Shops—the one projected onto the domed ceiling with red and orange lights. If I want to watch the seasons change, I'll go to the Bellagio Botanical Gardens, where a staff of 140 horticulturalists changes them twenty times faster than Mother Nature ever could. And while we're at it, why travel all the way to Europe just to see the Eiffel Tower, Arc de Triomphe, Piazza San Marco, Bridge of Sighs, Statue of David, or Colosseum when you can drive to Vegas and see them all in twenty minutes—along with the Statue of Liberty and the Sphinx?†

So many things in Las Vegas are fake, from the celebrities at Madame Tussauds to the beach at Mandalay Bay, from the volcano that erupts every hour at a hotel named (what else?) Mirage to the showgirls who paint their faces, pin on wigs, and simulate lesbian sex in Riviera's Crazy Girls. The city is filled with fakers, from celebrity impersonators to magicians. From casino hosts who tell high rollers that they'd "be happy to" oblige their most obnoxious, demeaning requests to gambling addicts who tell their spouses they don't have gambling problems. From strippers who, for a price, will

---

* Runner-up: Rainforest Cafe, 2nd Runner-up: Magic Kingdom's Jungle Cruise.
† Runner-up destination choice: Epcot's World Showcase.

shed their clothes and pretend that everything you say is charming and hilarious to escorts who, for a price, will pretend that everything you say is charming and hilarious and then shed their clothes, and then sleep with you.

No wonder so many people hate Las Vegas.

I don't hate deception and deceivers, though. In fact, in a strange way I'm drawn to them. I've always been drawn to them. I've always tried to learn their tricks and understand the psychology behind why they work. Not because I want to pull the tricks myself, but because I'm afraid of falling victim to them. And after the whole Elena/Solano situation went down, my innate fear multiplied:

I'm terrified of being conned and I don't want to be taken advantage of—not now, not ever. I don't want to buy a lemon, and I don't want to buy stock in the next Enron. I don't want to join a Ponzi scheme or vote for the next Randy "Duke" Cunningham. I don't want to wake up one morning with a strange, sneaking suspicion that I've been lied to and cheated on. In short, I don't want to be made the fool. And, obviously, I don't want anything like what happened to Elena to ever happen to me.

I don't think I was being overly paranoid. If you stop and think about how much deception there is in the world—in business, in advertising, in media, in politics, in romance—I think you'll agree that my fear was justified.

And that I had to learn to protect myself.

I might not remember everything from Professor Lewis's Consumer Protection class, but I do remember that much. I remember that the only one who can protect me, ultimately, is me.

And what better place to cultivate this protection than Las Vegas, the deception capital of the world? And what better time than now, before I got myself into a situation I couldn't fix, avoid, or escape?

So as my fellow law school graduates went off to Europe to "find themselves,"★ I headed to Las Vegas to meet deceivers, befriend them, watch them in action, learn from their tricks, and learn to protect myself.

Getting away from Elena and Solano was just the icing on the cake.

Hunter S. Thompson drove to Las Vegas at 100 miles per hour in a rented Chevy convertible carrying "two bags of grass, seventy-five pellets of mescaline, five sheets of high-powered blotter acid, a salt shaker half-full of cocaine, and a whole galaxy of multi-colored uppers, downers, screamers, laughers, and also a quart of tequila, a quart of rum, a case of Budweiser, a pint of raw ether, and two dozen amyls." I drove to Las Vegas at the speed limit in my mom's SUV, carrying a dozen dress shirts, a dozen ties, a couple boxes of kitchen supplies and toiletries, a briefcase full of magic tricks, my laptop, and my mom. I suppose it'd be fairer to say my mom

---

★ I'm pretty sure this is code for do drugs.

was carrying me, as she did most of the driving, which allowed me to focus on more important things like playing Mario on my Nintendo DS, playing Final Fantasy on my Nintendo DS, and complaining about my mom's driving.

We spent all but two nights of our weeklong cross-country journey at a Holiday Inn Express. Each hotel had the exact same layout, so after each day of travel we were never completely sure we hadn't been driving in a circle. Turns out we hadn't; we arrived in Las Vegas on a Thursday afternoon in late September and booked a room at the Palms Resort and Casino, the neo-retro twentysomething Mecca featured on MTV's *The Real World: Las Vegas,* back when people still watched *The Real World.*

Some people say that MTV (and VH1 and E!) and the commercials they run present female viewers with an impossible standard of beauty and youth. They do this, the argument goes, so women feel perpetually inadequate and insecure, which keeps them buying and buying in the hopes of achieving the unachievable, of becoming one of those TV women who, ostensibly, have no real-world counterpart. Ostensibly they're a myth.

There's a gaping hole in that theory, and if you spend some time at the Palms, you'll spot it. You'll spot it walking by you every few seconds. The supposedly impossible standard of female beauty is not only possible, not only achievable, but also *has been* achieved by half the women in the place. I'm not even talking about the cocktail waitresses, bartenders, and hostesses; I'm talking about the guests. Since its *Real World* heyday, the Palms has replenished itself with a new crop of beautiful girls in skimpy dresses.

The point I'm trying to make is, my God, there were a lot of attractive women at this place. Like the blonde and the redhead in the food court, sitting at a table for four.

"Are those two hookers?" my mom asked as we picked up our trays from the Panda Express counter.

"I don't know. Let's go find out. They look like they could use some company. . . ."

3. Ridiculousness Is in the Eye of the Beholder

Las Vegas doesn't have a very active chapter of the Society of American Magicians (SAM) or the International Brotherhood of Magicians (IBM). Las Vegas doesn't need one. Las Vegas has Gary Darwin's magic club. It's got no restrictions, membership fees, or rules of order. For Darwin, it's all about the magic.

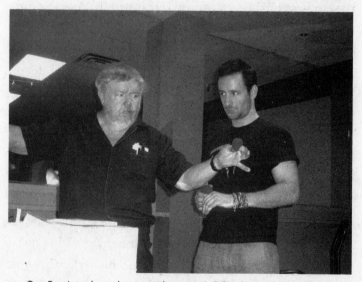

Gary Darwin teaches me how to vanish a sponge ball, for what must be the tenth time.

Darwin's club meets every Wednesday in the back room of Boomers, a dive bar just west of the Strip that pleasantly tolerates the magicians.

"Magicians don't drink much, is the problem," the bartender told me. "Guess they need their hands for other things."

The two non-magicians to my right laughed. I'd assumed the bartender was referring to sleight-of-hand maneuvers, but the laymen clearly thought she meant . . . something else. The guy to my left, an older conjurer in Velcro shoes, must have thought the same: "I was doing magic long before you were born," he said, "and let me tell you: I've heard better insults than that."

I figured Darwin's club was the ideal place to begin the process of integrating myself into Las Vegas's community of professional deceivers. And I was right; I felt at home with the other prestidigitators. In one night I met a dozen other magicians in their twenties, a dozen pros in their thirties, forties, and fifties, and a handful of former pros in their sixties, seventies, and even eighties. Some magicians came to Darwin's magic club to try out their new tricks and try to sell their old ones, others came for the friendship, and most came for both.

Since moving to Las Vegas a half century ago, Darwin has worked at the Flamingo, Desert Inn, Caesars Palace, and MGM Grand. He told me that he's invented over five hundred magic tricks, that he writes a book every month, and that he was the first person to do a straightjacket escape underwater. If you get the chance to meet the man he'll tell you all this himself, a minute or two after you shake his formidable hand. Then he'll pull out a plastic thimble or red sponge ball and show you a series of appearances and disappearances that will continue until (1) you ask him to show you a coin trick or (2) an attractive woman walks into the room.

Most of the women in attendance worked as magicians' assistants, like Shedini* (who worked with Jason Byrne) and Mistie (who works cruise ships with her husband, Tyler). But there were also two or three non-performing girlfriends—women whose lot in life is to select playing cards until their thumbs blister. I caught Darwin performing his thimble sequence before one of these non-magician girlfriends. Halfway through the routine, the woman went into a terrible coughing fit.

"Do you know any cough jokes?" Darwin asked her.

"No."

"Jokes are the best way to diffuse tension. If you go around coughing like that, you should have a cough joke ready to go. A good joke can get you out of any situation."

"I have asthma," she explained, clearly offended.

Darwin replied, "If you want to work on the Strip, you'll have to think up a better line than that."

Darwin and two of the younger magicians set up

---

* Her legal name, changed from Jessica.

twenty or thirty chairs, and little by little the magicians sat down in them. Darwin left the room and reentered wearing a blue blazer.

"Ladies and gentlemen," he began, "I'm pleased to inform you that we have a special guest with us tonight. It's amazing he's here, especially when you consider that he's been dead for over a decade. Ladies and gentlemen: George Burns."

Darwin had hired a George Burns impersonator.

Burns took a drag of his wooden prop cigar, adjusted his thick glasses, and said, "It's great to be here at Boomers tonight. But at my age, it's great to be anywhere. I'm a hundred and twelve. I'm getting old. I know I'm getting old because when I bend down to tie my shoe I think, I think, what else can I do as long as I'm down here?"

It took me a second, but I figured out that the impersonator was the guy from the bar with Velcro shoes. His voice was spot on, and if he had let his hair go gray, his appearance would have been, too.

"I was going to sing 'Young at Heart,' but before I went on, Gracie told me that this was some sort of magic club and that I should perform a magic trick for all of you."

Burns pointed at Darwin, who handed him a Magic Coloring Book, a trick I used to do at kids' birthday parties.

"I'm going to try my best not to screw this one up,

but I must admit: I have been drinking. It only takes me one drink to get drunk. The thing is, I can never remember if it's the thirteenth or fourteenth."

Burns placed the prop cigar in his breast pocket, lit end down, and flipped through the coloring book, showing all the pages blank.

"Some magicians use a magic wand, and others use magic fairy dust. I use both."

Burns waved the cigar over the coloring book like a magic wand.

"And now the dust."

He sprinkled some imaginary ashes.

"Now look."

He flipped through the book again. The pages were filled with black-and-white line drawings. This drew huge, sarcastic gasps from the audience of magicians, the sarcasm stemming from the Magic Coloring Book's simplicity. It's probably the easiest-to-perform parlor trick.

"And now, a little more fairy dust."

He sprinkled again and flipped through the book again. All the line images were filled with bright, vivid colors.

Wild applause.

"I'm so glad that worked. The truth is, I feel nervous performing magic before all of you. I don't like being deceptive. I like being honest. Life is all about honesty. If you can fake that, you've got it made."

After the show, Burns told me what separates his act from those of his competitors: "I know how to cater to my audience—that's so important when you're doing stand-up. If I were performing before a group of guys your age, I wouldn't do George Burns; I'd do Columbo."*

I moved from the bar to a nearby table, where three forty-something magicians were drinking beer, practicing card moves, and talking shit about Criss Angel.

"It's not his ego that gets to me," said a bearded conjurer. "It's that he tries to make every single trick he does the biggest, fastest, most dangerous trick in the history of magic—like he did with his metamorphosis. *That's* when he lost all credibility with me. Copperfield at least waited a year or two between each big trick— Statue of Liberty, the Bermuda Triangle, Niagara Falls. He gave people a chance to get excited about them. Angel just blows through them one after another, but he still tries to build each one up as if it's the Statue of Liberty."

According to the A&E network, Angel's TV show, *Mindfreak,* "stretches the boundaries of reality and belief in each thrilling episode as world-renowned mystifier Criss Angel executes incredible illusions, death-defying escapes, fearless demonstrations and astonishing physical feats." Season Two, Episode Ten—the "metamorpho-

---

* NBC dropped *Columbo* four years before I was born.

sis" episode that the bearded magician had cited—began the same way that all *Mindfreak* episodes do, with the following (self-defeating) words of caution:

WARNING

The stunts and illusions performed on this program were designed and tested by Criss Angel, a highly-trained professional. These demonstrations are extremely dangerous and should not be attempted by anyone, anywhere, at any time.

"Metamorphosis," says Angel at the start of the episode, "the ultimate transportation. No one does it faster. But tonight, my metamorphosis almost turns deadly."

Before I discuss whether the illusion actually turned "almost deadly," let me say that Angel performs some irrefutably dangerous tricks on *Mindfreak*. The "stunt" pieces in particular, like his helicopter body suspension. Of course, he and his team do everything they can to make these illusions appear even more dangerous than they really are, but many of them are still plenty dangerous.*

---

* I'd liken Criss's *Mindfreak* illusions to professional wrestling matches; the matches might be "fixed," but the danger is real. In the past decade sixty-five professional wrestlers have died premature deaths and countless more have suffered gruesome injuries. For example, in May of 1999, during a live Pay-Per-View event, as Owen Hart (the younger brother of Bret "Hitman" Hart) was being lowered to the ring by harness and rappel line, the early-release mechanism triggered and the young wrestler fell seventy-eight feet to the mat. He died almost instantly, from internal bleeding and blunt chest trauma. Another example: In October of '99, D'Lo Brown powerbombed Darren Drozdov. Apparently Drozdov's shirt was loose and Brown couldn't get a good grip on it. Drozdov landed on his head and fractured two discs. After extensive surgery at Nassau County Medical Center, Drozdov was left paralyzed from the neck down.

Metamorphosis is among the most frequently performed stage illusions. In it, the magician's assistant ties the magician in a cloth sack and then inside a crate. The assistant climbs on top of the crate and raises a blanket over her head. When the blanket is lowered, it's the magician who's standing on top of the box. He unties the trunk, removes the lid, unties the bag inside, and reveals his assistant.

So how does Criss turn this straightforward switcharoo into an allegedly "almost deadly" fiasco?

With fire.

Cut to downtown Las Vegas, Fremont Street.

A crowd of thousands has gathered around an assembled stage. The crowd chants, *"We want Criss! We want Criss!"*

Criss emerges and asks the audience, *"Are you ready?! Are you ready, Las Vegas?!"*

The crowd's cheers are definitive; Las Vegas is ready.

Criss jumps into the sack, inside the crate. Two men in black shirts tie the sack shut and then close the trunk. Criss's assistant, a short girl wearing denim booty shorts, a white tank top, and a painted-on Zorro mask, joins the men onstage. She climbs on top of the box and takes a few deep breaths, preparing herself for what's about to come.

The crowd counts backward from three and a wall of flames erupts from the metal cans set up before the trunk.

The fire lasts just a split second, and when it's gone Criss is standing on top of the box. He jumps off the crate and thrusts his hands into the air. He removes the box top and unties the bag inside. His assistant springs out of the bag and thrusts her hands up, too.

But then things take a turn.

The tape goes to slo-mo and Criss's assistant runs backstage.

Something is wrong.

Cut to Criss: "After the fire went off, I do my power pose"—he demonstrates his power pose—"and then you see me come forward for a second. I thought I was going to black out. The explosion that night was absolutely insane. It was huge. I knew I was slightly burned, but my first concern was Melanie. . . . When we got back to my RV, I noticed that my skin was really red. But we feared that Melanie got the worst of it, so we called the paramedics."

The episode ends as the paramedics cart Criss's assistant away in an ambulance.

Now, here was the magicians' consensus (myself included) on Angel's "almost deadly" metamorphosis: The assistant was fine. No second-degree redness, pinkness, or swelling. No third-degree whiteness or char. Absolutely no evidence whatsoever that she was truly burned.

"Why couldn't he just do the damn trick and get on

with it?" the bearded magician wanted to know. "He did it well, actually. Faster than the Pendragons."

The guy went on to criticize Criss for his use of camera editing and stooges. He seemed to be criticizing Criss for being deceptive in presenting his deceptions.

I had to speak up. Not to defend Criss, but to make clear that Criss wasn't the only TV magician using those kinds of tricks.

"But it's different with Criss," the bearded magician protested.

"How so?" I asked.

"Well . . . Criss is really bad at it."

Of course, the public at large disagreed. In late 2008, around the time I arrived in Las Vegas, Criss Angel was on top of the world—figuratively, yes, but literally, too: He levitated five hundred feet above the Luxor pyramid's point on the *Mindfreak* Season Three premiere. Angel's professional success was rivaled only by his romantic success. In mid-2007, he and model-turned-actress Cameron Diaz attended the VH1 Rock Honors together. And then, shortly after Angel's estranged wife accused Diaz of breaking up their marriage, Angel was spotted dancing with Pam Anderson at Luxor. In 2008 Angel dated the reigning Miss Nevada, and later that year he began dating reality television star Holly Madison, Hugh Hefner's ex-girlfriend. Angel was walking on water.

But then a snag. Angel's stage show, *BeLIEve,* was scheduled to open at the Luxor on October 10. But it got pushed back. According to Cirque du Soleil spokeswoman Anita Nelving, the decision to postpone the opening was made after a "lion's den" meeting, during which the Cirque creative directors determined that the show was not quite ready to go public. All Cirque shows go through this process, Nelving explained.

Cirque du Soleil had spent $100 million on *BeLIEve,* and Angel was given a fifty-two-hundred-performance ten-year contract. He was billed as the show's "co-writer, illusions creator and designer, original concept creator, and star." In a Cirque du Soleil promotional video, Angel said, "The truth of the matter is, expect the unexpected because this show is beyond my wildest fantasy. It is beyond anything I could even comprehend."*

A girl wearing the longest fake eyelashes I've ever seen approached our table and said, "Are you guys going to actually see Criss's show, or are you just going to sit around talking shit about it?"

"Probably just sit around talking shit," the bearded guy admitted.

"I don't think we met," I said to the girl. "I'm Rick."

"Mel."

"You look familiar."

---

* Come on, *that's* funny: a show so convoluted that *even the guy who wrote/created/designed/originated* it can't "comprehend" it.

"Have you seen Jeff McBride's show?" she asked.

"No."

"Kevin James?"

"Nope."

"Well, I assist them. Want to see?"

Before I could answer, Mel rolled back her sleeves and pulled up one of her pant legs to display her bruise collection. Yellow, brown, red, purple—those were the colors I found on her limbs.

"And you?" she said. "You're a magician?"

"Yep."

"Professional?"

"Not anymore. I used to do kids' shows, then table-hopping at Red Robin. Lately I've been doing some magic Internet videos, but that's about it."

"So what do you do then?"

"I just graduated from law school."

"So you're a lawyer."

"Technically, yes. I passed the Illinois Bar and the ethics test and got a certificate that says I'm a lawyer. But I haven't started practicing."

"So you don't do anything. Gotcha. How long are you going to be here for?"

"Vegas? Four or five weeks—tops."

"Do you have a place yet?" Mel asked.

"I put a posting on craigslist today."

"I'm only asking because my friend Oxana is looking

for a roommate. I'll introduce you two on Friday. You'll like her."

"What makes you say that?"

"All guys like her. . . ."

At 2:30 A.M., three of the magicians from Darwin's magic club and I drove to Arizona Charlie's, a locals casino, for "breakfast." Alex, twenty-four, and Michael, nineteen, had recently moved to Las Vegas with hopes of working the Strip. And given how they picked up the intricacies of the torn-and-restored card trick fifty-six-year-old Steve "Tiny" Daly was teaching them, I'd say they had a fighting chance.

Daly works with a lot of the young magicians who move to Las Vegas. He gives them access to his thousand-volume magic book library, full use of his thousand-piece illusion collection, and all the professional advice and personal guidance they could ever want. Two other interesting details about him: He weighs 450 pounds and performs in drag.

Needless to say, Daly had some great war stories:

"A couple of years ago, I got a call from some woman's secretary who asked me to come to the VIP section of TAO and impersonate Cher, as a birthday gift for her boss's husband. She said her boss would give me a thousand bucks for four minutes. I asked if she wanted me to bring a midget who does Sonny. She asked, 'How much?'

and I said, 'Half price. Fifteen hundred total.' Get it? 'Cause he's a midget? Anyway, fast-forward an hour or two. Me and Sonny go onstage, and we see who the secretary's boss was: Britney Spears. It was K-Fed's birthday."

"How'd the show go?" I asked.

"Britney loved us. She called me over for a hug, and then she wanted pictures, and then she wanted me to sit next to her—which I did. She was pregnant at the time, so I made sure she drank only water."

Daly had plenty of suggestions for Alex and Michael, the up-and-comers: "I know a hundred guys your age going for the same slot. They all do the same act. Birds, fire, boxes . . . You've got to be different. You've got to think of something original. Something without fire, without birds that shit everywhere, and without confetti. You don't want showgirls slipping on your mess and you don't want any fire code violations. Find something clean and different and the work will come to you."

"I sing and play the guitar," Michael offered. "I always wanted to combine my music with my magic."

"Now that," said Daly, "just might work."

We discussed advertising fees, booking procedures, and business models for about two hours. I asked Daly why he was so generous with his time.

"How many old fat guys do you know?" he responded.

I couldn't think of any.

"Exactly," he continued. "I'm fifty-six. If you look at the statistics, I've got about a year or two left to live. I could spend that time performing, but if I spend it with you, with the next generation, I mean, my work will go on a lot longer. I live vicariously through other magicians. Besides, if I were to put on a tux and do a suave, macho dove routine like Lance Burton—and believe me, I'd love to—people would laugh and go, 'Does he know he's fat?' You have to do what works."

Daly told us his plans for starting up a four-year Magic College. The first two years would cover the basics: misdirection, staging, costuming; the second two would be spent developing each student's individual act.

"That's the legacy I'd like to leave. But like I said, time is running out."

He handed Michael and Alex and me Keno crayons and told us to flip our paper place mats over.

"How long do you think you're going to live?" Daly asked us. "Write that number down. And how old are you right now? Write that number next to it and then subtract the two. Now show me what you got."

Michael wrote: "$90 - 19 = 71$."

"Seventy-one," Daly said, "You've got seventy-one more Christmases. You've got seventy-one more springs to watch the flowers bloom. Time moves faster than you think. If you really do want to take the Strip by storm, you've got to start right away—we're talking tomorrow."

Michael nodded solemnly. He'd gotten the message.

"How about you, Rick?"

I showed Daly my place mat: "150 − 26 = 124."

Daly rolled his eyes.

"I factored in advances in medical technology," I explained.

The 450-pound man who impersonates Cher for a living said this to me: "You're ridiculous."

Before we left the restaurant, I asked Daly what drove him to perform in drag. He asked me a question in return: "Did you ever watch *Here's Lucy*?"

"As a matter of fact, I did. That's the one after *The Lucy Show*—with Mr. Mooney."

He looked shocked.

"Back in middle school, I had insomnia and they'd show it on Nick at Nite," I explained.

"Then maybe you remember this episode: Lucy and Mr. Mooney go to see Phyllis Diller perform at a charity event. After the show the two go backstage and meet some guy named Jim Bailey, who says he's an impressionist. Lucy asks, 'Who do you impersonate?' and Bailey launches into Diller. It was Bailey the whole time. Mr. Mooney practically has a heart attack."

"So that inspired you."

"I saw that episode when I was young, and it made a huge impression on me. It made the magic I was doing unimpressive by comparison. Getting somebody to be-

lieve you're a totally different person—now *that's* deception. It's exhilarating. You should try it sometime."

"Maybe I will," I replied.

I was just being polite. At the time, I couldn't actually
see myself convincing anybody I was a different person.
Then again, at the time I also couldn't see myself staying in Las Vegas for longer than a couple of weeks. . . .

4. Rick Lax's 100 Percent Foolproof System for Sneaking into Nightclubs Without Paying Cover, Picking Up Beautiful Women in Under Forty-five Minutes, and Writing Overblown Chapter Titles

Before I met Mel's friend Oxana, a twenty-five-year-old six-foot-one-and-a-half Russian dancer, everything I knew about showgirls came from the movie *Showgirls*. Before Oxana met me, she'd never seen the movie.

She lived two miles west of the Strip with her creepy Sphynx cat, Nuzzlemuffin.

"He only *looks* like he doesn't have fur," she told me.

And what, that makes him *less* creepy?

Her apartment's walls were painted with bright reds and brighter oranges. It's how I imagined a narcoleptic would paint her house to stay awake. Oxana used to rent her extra room to a male dancer nicknamed Scottie.

"Once he woke me up with his music at like five A.M.,

and I went downstairs and opened the door to the garage and he was dancing on my car. Two guys were making out on the couch, and another guy was doing lines off the washing machine. It was a last-straw situation."

"I'd make such a boring housemate to you," I said.

"That'd be fantastic, but I doubt it. If it's not coke, it's something else. Everybody's got a vice."

"I don't."

"The most dangerous people are the ones who think they don't have vices."

"What's your vice?" I asked.

"I don't have any vices," she deadpanned. "So how long do you need the room for?"

"Not long. Just a month or so. Don't think of me as a potential roommate; think of me as a paying houseguest."

"You'll be here longer—you'll see. The city sucks people in. Nobody under thirty moves out of Vegas."

"What sucked you in?"

"I came here with a friend who was auditioning for two of the shows. The day of the first audition, she convinced me to go with her. I got the gig and she didn't. Been here ever since. So, you like it?"

"Sure, I've always loved Vegas."

"My place, I mean."

"Yeah, I do like it, but I'm going to check out a few other places with my mom today. I'll let you know by tonight."

By that point, I'd already decided I wanted to live with Oxana. Just negotiating.

"Fair enough," she said. "And speaking of tonight, if you don't have dinner plans, my friend Inessa and I are going to Sensi for dinner. It's at Bellagio. You're welcome to join us."

"Yeah, that'd be great. Thanks."

I used Oxana's downstairs bathroom before I left. Next to the sink sat a framed photo of two naked women, their hair dripping wet, their bodies slathered in baby oil. They hugged each other, breasts pressed against breasts. Their faces pointed toward the camera with serious, sensual expressions. The black-haired one on the right had a bob haircut and lots of eye shadow. The one on the left was Oxana.

"That's Inessa on the right," Oxana told me. "You'll meet her tonight, but don't get excited; she's married. And you're too short for me, so that won't be an issue, either, yes?"

"Yes."

As I opened the front door to leave, Oxana said this to her cat: "Nuzzlemuffin! You're getting a new daddy!"

"We'll see," I said. "See you at Bellagio."

Hotels like Bellagio are the biggest players in the Las Vegas deception game, and the deception starts early on. Example: in the mid-nineties, when casino mogul Steve

Wynn was creating the Bellagio, he wanted Chanel, Gucci, Prada, Hermès, Fred Leighton, Armani, and Tiffany to open stores at the hotel. Problem was—this according to *Wall Street Journal* reporter Christina Binkley—back in the 1990s, when most people thought of the Vegas fashion scene, they thought of clothing like that worn by my Panda Express dinner companions. So none of the designers wanted to sign on first.

Steve Wynn and his retail executive Frank Visconti were facing the classic Project Sign-On Dilemma,★ but Visconti found a way around it. When one of the designers asked him whether Chanel had signed on, he said, "Yeah. I'm looking at his signature." Visconti later explained to Binkley, "I had to lie to get the first guy." The lie worked: Wynn got all the designers he was after and then some.

Another example: With designers in place, Wynn prepared for Bellagio's grand opening. The mogul hired a philharmonic orchestra to underscore the twelve-hundred-nozzle dancing fountains' debut with the sounds of Debussy's "Clair de Lune" (the song from the end of *Ocean's Eleven*) and Copland's *Appalachian Spring* (the song from everything else).† Problem was, with the fountains going full blast, guests couldn't hear the music

---

★ The Project Sign-On Dilemma occurs when a producer is trying to attract big-name movie stars to an orphan script and each star says he'll only sign on if another star has already signed on.

† Except for clashes between good and evil, which are set to Orff's *Carmina Burana*.

over the sound of the splashing water. So the orchestra pulled an Ashlee Simpson★—the symphonic equivalent of lip-syncing.†

I arrived at Bellagio around 8:00 P.M. and spotted Oxana and Inessa from across the casino. Kinda hard to miss. As they walked from the valet parking area to the lobby, every head turned. Mostly up.

"He's cute," said Inessa to Oxana. "Are you going to keep him?"

I don't think she was saying I'm attractive. I think she was making a height joke.‡

★ On October 23, 2004, Ashlee Simpson (who was specifically manufactured to have an un-manufactured image. The persona her vast team of handlers picked for her was that of handler-free autonomy. Unlike Christina, Britney, sister Jessica, and the other lyric bombshells of the new millennium, whose phoniness, the story went, was symbolized by their blond hair, Ashlee was a down-to-earth brunette! [At least, she was when I first wrote that last sentence.] Of course, to get this look, she had to dye her hair from blond to brunette. And that wasn't Ashlee's only physical transformation. In 2006, right after Ashlee told *Marie Claire* that she had "had it with Hollywood's twisted view of feminine beauty," she got a nose job. I mean *right after*—as in before the issue hit the stands. Ashlee's fans don't seem to mind the hypocrisy. Her 2008 album debuted at number four on the Billboard 200 and sold more than two hundred thousand copies.) was scheduled to perform two songs on *Saturday Night Live*. She got through the first song, "Pieces of Me," without a hitch, but when the band started playing her second song, "Autobiography," her prerecorded "Pieces of Me" vocal track started playing again . . . before she got the microphone to her mouth. Ashlee did a jig and then walked off the stage as her band played on. Cut to commercial. In the last minute of the live broadcast Ashlee said, "I'm so sorry. My band started playing the wrong song and I didn't know what to do." Ashlee implied that she made a foolish snap decision (to lip-sync the song) only *after* her band started playing the wrong song. But obviously the decision to lip-sync the song was made in advance. Two days later on *Total Request Live* Ashlee claimed she was suffering from acid reflux.

† This paragraph was much more damning when I first wrote it before Yo-Yo Ma and Itzhak Perlman Ashlee Simpsoned the Obama inauguration ceremony.

‡ I want to mention that I'm not short in the objective sense; I'm five-eleven.

"I'm going to try," Oxana replied. "He hasn't told me if he's staying yet."

Here's how I greeted Inessa: "I've seen you naked."

"Either you've been in Oxana's bathroom or I was plastered, because I don't remember you at all."

"Behave, Inessa—at least until Rick writes me a rent check."

We walked through the casino, under Dale Chihuly's two-thousand-flower glass sculpture, and through the botanical garden, which at the time featured giant Venus flytraps, a working cider mill, a real one-thousand-pound pumpkin, and a talking apple tree (which I'm pretty sure was fake). We arrived at Sensi and were seated next to the glass-walled center kitchen. Inessa asked us whether we'd tried the ginger ale before, but before we could answer she told the waitress, "We're getting the ginger ale. Everybody's getting ginger ale."

I might have resented Inessa's audacity . . . if the ginger ale didn't taste so delicious. Turns out ginger ale is supposed to taste like ginger.

Inessa ordered sweet chili asparagus sauce and goat-cheese donuts for the whole table, too. Also good decisions.

"How'd you two meet?" I asked at one point.

"At *Fashionistas*," Oxana said. "The old show at Aladdin."

Fashionistas, which closed in 2008, was produced by

John Stagliano, a man made famous for inventing a genre of pornographic film known as "gonzo."

"You should have seen it," Inessa said. "We did this great routine where we were all S&M horses. This guy, this character in the show—it had a plot: boy-meets-girl sort of thing—was trying to turn this girl on, so he left her a porn DVD, and we were acting out what was on the DVD."

"Long story short," Oxana said, "we had to dance around with these rubber tubes in our mouths."

"*Got* to dance around with tubes in our mouths," Inessa corrected.

"You mean a *bit*?" I asked.

"Yeah," said Inessa, "a *bit*. And after two months of dancing in the show, I figured out that *that* was what was giving me this nasty rash on the corners of my mouth. Didn't bother me as much as it bothered the guy I was dating at the time."

"Once you've galloped for a living," I asked Inessa, "where do you go from there? I mean, what's left?"

"Not much. I've been in Vegas ten years now. No surprises left. Nothing new under the sun. So what brought you here?"

"Right now I'm studying deception."

"In school?"

"No, they let me graduate. Just studying deception for fun."

"And . . . how are we supposed to believe that?" Inessa asked.

"Pass me another donut and I'll prove it."

Inessa stabbed one with her fork and handed it over. I broke off a bite-size chunk, swallowed it, and opened my mouth wide and showed it empty.

After a couple seconds, Oxana said, "Okay, I'll bite" (pun intended?). "I don't get it."

"During the Spanish Inquisition," I explained, "if they thought you were lying, they'd have you swallow a piece of bread or a piece of cheese, and if it got stuck in your throat, they knew you were. The thought was, lying makes you anxious and angst decreases saliva flow. And decreased saliva flow makes it more likely that a piece of food will get stuck in your throat."

"Wait a second," said Inessa. "How do we know you're not lying about that, too?"

"Lots of cultures believed the saliva thing," I said, totally avoiding her question. "In India, they'd have you chew dry rice and spit it out, and if they saw blood in it, they knew you were lying. And there's this Arab tribe called the Bedouin and they had you lick a hot iron, and if your tongue burned, they'd know you were lying."

Oxana frowned and said, "But anybody who had to touch their tongue to a hot iron would be nervous."

"She's a liar!" Inessa cried.

"Burn her!" I joined in.

"Burn Oxana!"

"Burn the witch!"

Oxana, Inessa, and I arrived at the JET nightclub around 12:30 A.M. JET opened at The Mirage in 2006, which means—let me grab my calculator here—the club is eighty-four in Vegas club years. JET plays dance, eighties, and house, and while I don't know what "house music" is, I know that it's cool to say you're tired of it—which, incidentally, I am. JET had four separate lines: one for nobodies, one for people on the list, one for "Girls Only," and one for VIPs. The lines snaked and weaved and did everything else lines could do except move forward.

"I feel so bad for the tourists," Oxana said.

"What do you mean?" I asked.

"Having to wait in the line, I mean. They fly here from across the world to wait around, basically. They spend more time in the lines than they do in the clubs. For most people, this is what Vegas nightlife is all about. But they don't realize that until they're actually stuck in the line. I could never be a tourist."

Oxana was right. The lines are awful. Next time you visit Las Vegas, stand outside JET for twenty minutes (or Tryst, or The Bank, or Pure, or XS, or TAO, or Haze) and check out the girls waiting in line. Note the Asians with long blond hair and the blondes with Asian tattoos. Note the pressed-up breasts, the petite frames, the tanned legs, the curves. And then remember: You're looking at the girls who *weren't* attractive enough to get into the club straightaway.

Back in Chicago, when my law school classmates and I debated which bar to patronize, our mantra was "some place with no cover." The cover we so desperately sought to avoid was usually five dollars, sometimes ten. *Why should we pay money for the privilege of paying for drinks?* we wondered. Well, if you want to get into JET and you're not on the list, aren't painfully attractive (and female), and don't have your own basic cable TV show, it will cost you twenty or thirty dollars, depending on the night and on your sex.★ Paying thirty dollars not only buys you the right to buy overpriced drinks; it also serves as your reward for waiting in line for an hour. Yes, you can avoid the line entirely by purchasing a front-of-the-line pass, but you'll still have to wait in the front-of-the-line-pass line, and it'll cost you fifty dollars.

Still, there's hope. In *Party like a Rock Star Even When You're Poor as Dirt,* Camper English offers these Darwinian tips on getting into a club without waiting in line:

> The taller you are, the better your chance of getting noticed over the top of the crowd. Wear platforms or your stripper heels.

★ One Saturday night at Haze, they wanted one hundred dollars for cover. Wasn't a holiday or anything.

If you got it, flaunt it. When your group of hot chicks approaches the door, they're going to let you all right in rather than make you all wait because of the one ugly dude.*

When approaching the club, arrange your posse in order of most to least sexy so that the bouncers will see the hot people first and (hopefully) let you all in.

Another way to dodge the line is by purchasing bottle service. For those of you over fifty, here's how bottle service works: A bartender goes to the grocery store and buys a bottle of, say, Patron Silver Tequila 750 ml for fifty dollars. Then the bartender gives the Patron to a "bottle girl" who walks it over to your table, opens it, and hands you a bill for five hundred dollars. Expected tip is one hundred dollars.†

If you want to get into a Vegas club without waiting in line and without buying bottle service, there's one last thing you can do: Tip the bouncer. This should go

---

* This doesn't apply at most Vegas nightclubs.

† Okay, I suppose there's a bit more to it: Along with the Patron, you get orange juice, pineapple juice, limes, salt, and a couch or two. So you're not really buying the booze; you're buying the real estate. You're buying the ability to approach girls and say, "My friends and I have a table. You're welcome to join us." You need to have this ability because local girls expect it. Local girls don't buy their own drinks—there's an unwritten policy against it. And to make sure they abide by this rule, local girls often leave their credit cards and cash at home. And then they walk around telling guys, "I didn't bring my credit card or money." That's part of the reason many clubs let local girls in for free; they help empty bottles, which then need to be replenished at five hundred dollars a pop.

without saying, but in case it doesn't, here goes: Twenty dollars ain't gonna cut it. How much you should tip depends on whether you're a guy or girl, and whether you're attractive or unattractive. From what I've heard, every bouncer has a price—and I say that with no disrespect. "Rob the Bouncer" says in his book *Clublife* that it's a bouncer's *job* to get as much money from you as he can:

> Making money at the door was a simple proposition. You took bribes. You solicited as many bribes as you could, as often as you could, for as much as you could possibly squeeze. When you stand in line outside of a nightclub, especially when the line is long, you're nothing but a dollar sign to the bouncers at the door. My job up front was to halt your forward progress—to find something, anything, I could use to justify preventing you from walking through the door. . . . If getting in actually means something to you, the only way it's going to happen is if you bite the bullet and fork over some cash.

Of course, Oxana had no plans to bribe or be squeezed: "I've done some gigs with one of the bartenders here, and I had her put me and Inessa on the list, but that was before I knew you were coming, and the thing is, it's so packed tonight, there's no way they're going to let you in with us. So go busy yourself for a bit, and then in a half hour I'll text you, and we'll meet up by the bathroom, and then we'll sneak you back in with us."

"Okay, but how?"

"You'll see. I've done this one before."

Forty-five minutes and one hundred dollars later— meaning I lost one hundred dollars at the poker table— Oxana sent me a text telling me to meet her by the bathroom. When I got there, she and Inessa were laughing wildly and exchanging high fives with bouncers at the door. Oxana spotted me and signaled for me to meet her and Inessa by the bathroom.

"These guys from Jersey kept buying us shots of beer," Inessa told me. "Is that what they do in Jersey? And we kept telling them not to buy us any more, and they kept on buying them, and they kept on doing it until we were like, *'We're not going to sleep with you,'* and even if we were, we're not going to after you bought us *beer shots*. Who *does* that?"

I pulled out my imaginary dictation machine and began to take a "note to self" regarding the purchase of beer shots, but Inessa slapped it out of my hand and it imaginary hit the floor and imaginary shattered.

"Common sense!" Inessa scolded.

"We're going to walk back to that bouncer," Oxana said, "the guy we were just talking with. You just stand behind us and don't say anything. Think you can handle that?"

"I'll try."

"Try to look bored," she added.

We approached the bouncer and I rolled my eyes, checked my cell phone, and imagined I was Paris Hilton.

"Hi again," Oxana said to the bouncer. "We thought we were on our way out, but our ride, Rick's brother, is still drinking coffee and sobering up in the sportsbook. Can we go back in until then?"

"You guys didn't get your hands stamped," the bouncer told all three of us.

"I know. I'm sorry," Oxana said. "It's just he really shouldn't be on the road right now, you know? Better safe than sorry."

"Gimme your hands."

By flirting with the bouncers as she walked out, Oxana ensured he'd remember her upon reentry. And then, when we were trying to get back in, she pointed to me early on, connecting me with her and Inessa. Bouncers don't pay much attention to random guys walking out of clubs. Nobody does. We all look the same to them. The bouncer must have assumed I'd left the club with them. And then the bit about wanting to avoid a drunk-driving situation—very impressive.

I "re"entered JET and was greeted with a neon green laser in my eyes and, a few minutes later, something on my shoe. Upon impact, I assumed the "something" was the contents of someone's drink, and technically I was right; some big guy vomited on my shoe. It wasn't chunky vomit like Elena's; it was the dark brown, bourbony kind—the kind that smells awful but doesn't look any different from, well, bourbon. It probably matched my shoes perfectly.★

I asked the closest bartender, a girl with bleached spiked hair and tattoos running up her left arm, for a glass of water.

"Some guy threw up on my shoe," I explained.

"I can't give you a glass," she replied. "Just a bottle."

"I don't want to *buy* it. I just *want* some tap water—to clean my shoes."

"How do I know you're not going to drink it?"

"Give me a piece of bread or cheese and I'll prove it."

"What the fuck are you talking about?"

"In the Spanish—"

Mid-factoid the bartender dropped her smile and turned away. She walked to two men in fancy suits standing a couple feet down. She took their drink order and then came back to me.

"Sorry, what were you saying?"

"Forget it. I really need some water, though. And I know you're not supposed to give out water 'cause it cuts into your sales, but some guy really did throw up on my shoe."

"If I give you the water, everybody is going to say they need some water to clean their shoes."

★ That's the only time I've ever been vomited on. I only mention this because you just got done reading the scene where I gave Elena the vomity bear hug and I don't want you to think that I'm constantly covered in vomit. I'm not. For instance, right now, as I type this footnote, I've got no vomit on me.

So, what, this girl thought I was going to walk up to every guy in the place and say, *Pssst! That bartender over there—the one with the spiky blond hair—if you go up to her and tell her that somebody vomited on your shoes, she'll give you a free glass of water. Swear to God. Pass it on!?*

"Can I just have a wet rag?" I asked.

"Fine."

The bartender set a damp rag in front of me and took another drink order.

Las Vegas nightclubs don't hire bartenders for their friendliness—nor for their ability to pour rum and lime juice into the same glass. Las Vegas nightclubs hire based on looks.

In 2007, a group of forty-to-sixty-five-year-old male Mirage bartenders, led by fifty-one-year-old plaintiff Robert Thomas, filed complaints with the Nevada Equal Rights Commission charging The Mirage with age and sex discrimination. The plaintiffs claimed they had been passed over for lucrative bartending jobs at JET. According to Thomas's attorney, "The Mirage is trying to attract a younger, hipper clientele, and in keeping with that they've effectively excluded these older workers who are equally qualified, if not more qualified, than these younger bartenders. There's no reason why these guys shouldn't be allowed to work in these bars."*

★ The plantiffs settled for twenty-five thousand dollars each.

Mirage created separate union contracts with JET, which allowed Light Group, the hospitality management company that hired the bartenders, to bypass union seniority rules and hire nonunion workers (who could later join the union). The Bartenders Union and Culinary Union are always doing battle with the casinos over age and sex discrimination issues. Grossly simplified, the unions want casinos to hire older guys; the casinos want to hire younger girls. And the casinos don't always try to hide this, either. A typical job description in the local newspaper classifieds section reads like this:

> The Imperial Palace is seeking Glamorous and Sexy Palace Princesses for the enhancement of our casino guests' entertainment experience. This position requires height in proportion to weight attributes and the ability to heighten our adult players' gaming experience through the use of alluring costumes and service of complimentary cocktails.★

Displeased several times over, I wiped the remnants of the regurgitated cocktail off my shoe and tossed the rag onto the rail at the end of the bar. Oxana found me, pointed at the spiky-haired bartender, and said, "That's

---

★ In case you couldn't tell, that's corporate-speak for no fatties.

Zella. She's the one who put our names on the list. Come on; let me introduce you."

Before I could tell Oxana we'd already met, Oxana got the girl's attention and officiated our awkward handshake.

"*You're* Oxana's friend?" she said. "Oh my God. I'm so sorry about the water thing. That was my boss behind the bar with me, and I just got in trouble this weekend for giving out drinks. And before *that* he was already pissed at me for this other thing—not work related, I mean not JET related—and I don't even know one hundred percent what the water policy actually is, but he was *right behind* me, and I didn't know what to do, and I'm really not a hard-ass like that. Tell him, Oxana."

"Zella's not a hard-ass," Oxana confirmed, still unsure of what we were talking about.

"I'm not. That's not me at all. I just—yeah, that's not me."

"What are you talking about?" Oxana said. I filled her in as Zella went off to mix a couple of cocktails for a group of Italian guys at the other end of the bar. Then she did a couple of shots with them.

"Was she being bitchy?" Oxana asked.

"I thought so at the time, but it sounds like she—"

"She just had this awful breakup. She found out that the guy she'd been dating for more than a year was working as an escort."

"And 'escort' is code, right? I mean, the guy was sleeping with the girls he was 'escorting' . . . ?"

"*Girls*? No. Women don't pay for that stuff. He was a gay escort."

Oh.

"But she was wearing that ring," I said. "It looked like a wedding ring."

"You can ask her about that when she gets back."

I'd only noticed her ring because so few girls in Vegas who work for tips wear wedding rings, regardless of whether they're married. The rings cut down on tips. If a Vegas cocktail waitress or bartender is wearing a ring on her ring finger, it's probably less an indicator of marital status than it is an indicator that she's sick of customers hitting on her.

When Zella returned, I asked her about the ring.

"It's a promise ring, *not* a wedding ring."

"You're pre-engaged?" I asked.

"Sort of. To Jesus."

My jaw dropped. It was a *virginity* promise ring.

"I'm not a virgin," she said. "I just revirginated myself. Very recently, actually. I'm not a Jesus Freak or anything. Used to be. Rears its head from time to time, like when you find out the guy you've been dating . . . never mind. Story for another time. Or maybe Oxana already told you? Anyway, I'm sorry about the water thing, and I want to . . . Hang on. . . ."

A guy in a suit standing behind the bar was tapping her on the shoulder. Same guy who had been behind her before. Her boss, presumably. She turned around, he gave her a look, and then he walked away.

"I've got to get back to work," Zella said to me. "Those guys down there need drinks. You're cute, by the way."

Didn't sound like a height joke that time.

When Zella got to the other end of the bar—two more shots with the Italian guys—Oxana explained, "She wants you to ask her out. And you should, right away."

"Why? Because she's on the rebound and would never date me otherwise?"

"No—well, *yes*—but more because you just moved here and you need to make some friends."

Fair enough.

"*And,*" Oxana continued, "I'm sure she used protection with her ex, if that's what you're thinking about."

"No, that's not what I'm thinking about," I lied. "Besides, she said she 'revirginated' herself."

"We'll see how long that lasts," Oxana said.

"So I'm supposed to ask her out *tonight*?"

"Don't be silly. You *never* ask an industry girl out while she's working. That *reeks* of tourist."

"Let's do this," I said. "When Zella walks back over here, laugh really hard like I just told the best joke in the world. And after a minute or two, ask her if she's going to come to my book reading."

"You're doing a book reading?"

"In a couple weeks, at the Town Square Borders."

"Why can't you just invite her yourself?" Oxana asked. "Tomorrow we can all get coffee or something."

"Because if you invite her for me, she'll think I'm famous *and* modest. Okay, she's coming back; laugh really hard, right now."

Oxana let out the biggest, fakest laugh in the history of modern hysterics.

"That sounds suspiciously like one of those 'laugh when she comes over here' laughs . . . ," Zella said.

And that time Oxana's laughter was genuine.

"So, are you coming to Rick's book reading?" Oxana asked, trying to keep a straight face.

"Rick didn't mention it."

"That's Rick for ya: famous *and* modest."

Zella passed me a cocktail napkin.

"Write down your number," she said.

I wrote it down and gave it to her.

"I'll text you later tonight so you have my number, too."

She never did.

Every summer, the *Photinus pyralis* fireflies light up the meadows and woodlands of North America. Look for them in May and June—but look carefully, they're only a centimeter long. When the male *Photinus* is in the mood, he flashes his tiny light every six seconds. If a female *Photinus* is interested, she flashes back on a two-second delay.

Enter the *Photuris* firefly.★ When a female *Photuris* spots a male *Photinus* flashing, she mimics the flash pattern of an interested female *Photinus,* and after a couple dozen flash cycles the male *Photinus* drops his pants and mounts the female *Photuris.*

Then she eats him.

The female *Photuris* is so consumed by devouring male *Photinus* fireflies that she often loses interest in mating with the male *Photuris.* To get any action the male *Photuris* is forced to mimic the mating call of the male *Photinus* just to get a hungry female *Photuris*'s attention.

Now, if fireflies can create that much romantic deception with pin-sized lights alone, imagine what human beings are capable of.

A couple days after I moved in with Oxana and sent my mom back to my dad and the Michigan cold, I asked Oxana what she looks for in a guy.

"Somebody honest," she said. She said that she'd dated liars and cheaters before and what she really wanted was "somebody who doesn't play games."

Most books that purport to turn regular guys into Pickup Artists (PUAs) advocate all sorts of game playing and deception, such as Tony Clink's *The Layguide:*

★ These names are similar but different. The first firefly—the one that flashes every six seconds when it's horny—is a *PhotINUs*. The second one is a *PhotURIs*.

How to Seduce Women More Beautiful Than You Ever Dreamed Possible (No Matter What You Look Like or How Much You Make), Brett Tate's *The Professional Bachelor: How to Exploit Her Inner Psycho,* and Mystery's *The Mystery Method: How to Get Beautiful Women into Bed.*

Here's one of the specific tactics PUA guru Mystery uses to get these beautiful women into bed:

> Take pictures of yourself in interesting situations. Active shots—you doing fun things. Goofing off at your workout place. Rock climbing. Partying with male friends and girls. In midair while Rollerblading. The bear shit from the bear you bumped into while hiking. The best photos will convey value as well as your identity. Also include a couple of boring out-of-focus pictures for realism. Put these photos in a developing envelope, as though you just picked them up from the store where they were developed today and you just happen to have them with you. . . . For each picture, tell a story. During this time, you can demonstrate preselection, social proof, or other DHVs [Demonstrations of Higher Value]. . . .

The photo routine is filled with deceptive elements. Mystery acts like he just got some photos developed when, in actuality, they've been developed for a while. He acts like he's carrying them around because he hasn't yet gotten the chance to set them down when in actuality he's carrying them around for the purpose of picking up women.

Now, I've never tried Mystery's photo routine out, but not because I have any moral qualms with it. I admit the routine is manipulative, but not necessarily in a bad way. I can picture Mystery using this technique to pick up a woman and then, at a later date, revealing to her what he did and why he did it. I can picture the girl having a good laugh about it.

That's not the case with other PUA "gambits," such as Tony Clink's "Rich and Famous Setup":

> Instead of approach, you have your wing move in on her and start chatting—without trying to pick her up. After a minute or two, have him call you over and introduce you. Say "Hi," but look a little uncomfortable and leave soon after. "Poor guy," your wing says. "Do not waste your time on him. Women hit on him all the time, but they're only after his money. He just gets so tired of it." She says, "Oh, he's rich?" "Unfortunately. And kind of famous, too."

The Rich and Famous gambit *might* lead to a phone number and it *might* lead to sex, but it will *definitely* lead to disappointment and resentment. Many romantic lies do.

Men commonly lie to women about their income, their status, and their possessions. We wear knockoff designer watches and fold hundred-dollar bills around singles. We're hardwired to pull these stunts because (1) women are attracted to men who can provide for potential offspring and (2) it's easier to act wealthy than it is to actually become wealthy.

Another deception: When picking up women, we act like we're not trying to pick up women. We understand that women steer clear of guys who are "on the prowl." On-the-prowl guys come off as desperate, and desperation is a turnoff. After all, people want what they can't have. If you saw a pair of pants folded up on the sidewalk you wouldn't think, *Hey, free pants!*; you'd think, *What the hell is wrong with those pants? Why did somebody leave those pants there? Is this some sort of setup? Am I on a hidden-camera show? Am I being framed for murder? Somebody get these pants away from me!*

Accordingly, PUAs have developed hundreds of nonthreatening, nonsexual conversation-starters. Take the Lint Opener in which a PUA approaches his "target"* with a piece of lint palmed in his hand, pretends to pluck it off her, and says, "How long has this been there? Do you always go out dressed like that?" Or take the Cologne Opener, in which the PUA sprays different scents on his wrists and asks his target which one she prefers.

---

* Sadly, this is the official PUA term.

Not all PUAs advocate this sort of deception. Take Matt Ardisson, aka Artisan, a featured panelist for the 2009 PUA World Summit.★ I met Artisan and his girl-friend at Peppermill, a twenty-four-hour diner with a flaming pool and ten-egg omelet selection, located right on Las Vegas Boulevard. If nothing else, I figured, a pickup artist such as Artisan would be able to tell me why Zella hadn't texted me as she'd promised.

"I don't even like using the term 'pickup artist,'" Artisan said. "I'm not against it; it just has a sleazy connotation. 'Pickup artist' sounds like 'scam artist' or 'con artist.' The whole pickup scene has a bad reputation. People think it's all about tricking women into bed. And for some guys, sure, it is, but for my students, it's about being genuine, being playful, being more comfortable in your skin, and building inner confidence. It's definitely not about lying."

"You recognize that you're in the minority here," I said.

"Sure, a lot of guys take the lying thing really far.

★ Taken from Artisan's Web site, TheAttractiveMan.com:

Tired of being alone? Sick of not getting the dates you want? Want more dating options? Learn the secrets of how to approach, attract, and "close" beautiful women anytime—anywhere. Take a stand! It's time to man-up and get your dating life in gear. The Attractive Man offers exclusive 1-on-1 coaching custom designed for YOU. We will teach you the secrets of being a Social Master. You'll never be caught not knowing what to say again! (Or how to say it.) You'll learn how to be more confident and in-teresting so women will always want to be around you. It's time to get the success you deserve!

There's a radio host who tells his listeners to go through trash cans near ATM machines, find the receipts with high balances, and use them as paper when you give a girl your phone number so women think you're rich. He says you should tell women you're a lawyer."

I laughed.

"Don't tell me *you* tell women you're a lawyer," Artisan said.

"Sometimes . . ."

"Yeah, I wouldn't recommend that. Just be honest. See, systems like the Mystery Method—the book, the game, the TV show—they teach guys to say things that aren't true. Like the opener: 'What do you think of David Bowie? Do you think he's hot?' Does the guy asking that really care if Bowie is hot? No. Of course not. And here's another example: 'I have a friend named Herman. Do you think that's a fuckable name?' Nobody has a friend named Herman, and nobody cares if it's a fuckable name. If you're going to ask a question, you should ask an honest one."

"And why's that?"

"You know, I used to use other people's stories—Mystery Method–type stuff. Here's an example: I'd say, 'There are these four girls, and they've got this house on the beach, and they want me to move in with them, but I'm not sure I should. I mean, they'd probably take over the bathroom and I'd have to shower in a truck stop. Plus, girls are way more sexual than guys, so what if I get date-raped?' See, in that story I'm subconsciously promoting the idea that girls like me and trust me. Plus I've got two jokes in there. And when I get to the line about girls being more sexual than guys, a lot of times a girl would comment on that, and the conversation would go from there."

"That sounds pretty good to me," I admitted.

"It is, but I don't use it anymore because if I do, if I tell that sort of lie, and if I do end up sleeping with the girl, eventually things are going to feel fake and the truth is going to come out. That's happened to me before. So now I teach guys to be genuine. If a girl is by herself at the mall, I tell guys it's better to walk up to her and say, 'You're cute. You get a high five,' or something straightforward and silly like that. That's not the best opener, but it's better than lying, and it's definitely better than doing nothing."

"Are there any times when you are deceptive?" I asked.

"Okay, I guess one thing I do is, if I'm telling a girl a story that happened two years ago, I might say that it happened a week ago. I still do that. So, yeah, that's a little deceptive. Actually, I won't even say it happened 'a week ago.' I'll say it 'just happened. . . .'"

I told Artisan about Zella and asked him what my next move should be.

"Yeah, that happens. Happens to the best of us. Not much you can do at this point. You just have to wait until she calls you. Sounds like she probably won't, though . . . so maybe we should try to meet some other people tonight."

We drove to LAVO, the restaurant/nightclub/ bathhouse at Palazzo, The Venetian's sister casino, and we ordered mojitos from the bar in the downstairs lounge area. I assumed that when I asked Artisan whether I could see him in action he'd tell me that he didn't like to perform before journalists, that he didn't like to talk to other women with his girlfriend around, that LAVO wasn't a good place to pick up women, or something like that. In other words, I assumed he'd make up an excuse not to do it. I assumed he wouldn't want to be rejected in front of some guy who might write about it.

I was totally wrong. When I said, "Can I see you work?" he leapt right into action. Didn't hesitate for a second.

He approached a nearby group of three cute Indian girls, one of whom was wearing a tiara. He asked Tiara Girl some question—I couldn't hear what it was—and then after she gave her answer he gave her a high five. Artisan's girlfriend and I were standing ten or fifteen feet away, so we didn't hear any of the conversation that followed, but we did watch as, one by one, the girls smiled. Twenty or thirty seconds into his set, he got a big hug from the cutest girl in the group. Then the girls walked upstairs to the club area.

"They said we should meet up with them upstairs a bit later," Artisan told me.

"What were you guys talking about?"

"Nothing really. I was just being friendly and silly. I asked the girl with the tiara when the big day was, but it turned out it was just her twenty-first birthday."

"And how'd you get the hug?" I asked.

"I don't know. She just sort of hugged me."

I couldn't tell if Artisan was being coy or approaching strangers truly was a naturally thoughtless activity for him. So I looked around the lounge and spotted two women sitting in the corner on one of LAVO's plush benches. Possibly a mother and daughter, probably on vacation. They looked like they were deep in conversation; they'd definitely sectioned themselves off from the rest of the crowd.

"How about them?" I said. "How would you approach a group like that? People who clearly want to be by themsel—"

Artisan leapt into action again. He plopped himself down next to the older one (in her late forties or early fifties) and started talking. And once again, within a few seconds, the women were smiling.

After two minutes, I approached and sat down next to Artisan.

"Who's your friend?" the young one asked.

"This is Rick the Writer."

"What are you writing about, Rick the Writer?" she asked.

"Deception. I actually just interviewed Artisan here. He teaches men how to pick up women. We were talking about that and about how it's important to be honest when you do it."

As the words came out of my mouth, the irony hit me: *There's no chance in hell these women are going to believe me. They'd sooner believe I have a potentially fuckable friend named Herman or a pending offer to live with four girls on the beach.*

Sure enough, when I stopped talking, the two started laughing.

"So, what, this is some sort of tag-team technique for meeting women?" the older lady asked. "One guy pretends to be a writer and the other guy pretends to be Will Smith from *Hitch*?"

"It's true!" I said.

"Sure it is," the older one said. "Next you're going to tell my daughter you're a lawyer, like that guy with the piercings over there."

"Why does every guy go around saying they're—," Artisan stated to say.

"I *am* a lawyer!" I volunteered, realizing I had nothing to lose at that point.

The women rolled their eyes.

"Rick and I should get going," Artisan said. And then he pulled me up and we rejoined his girlfriend.

"Maybe a less straightforward approach would work better for you," Artisan said.

The club at Luxor used to be named after the Egyptian sun god, Ra, but now it's named after me.★ Going to LAX is kind of like going to hell, but not in a bad way; the club has a hell motif is all. Oxana and I passed under the gothic wrought-iron gate erected before a pair of red curtains and then ascended and descended the stairs into the club's main room—an explosion of black, red, metal, and strobe. We ordered Negronis, settled into a spot between the bar and front entrance, and looked for a girl with whom I could attempt a "less straightforward approach."

And then we found one.

"If you keep staring at her," Oxana said, "you're going to spill your drink on yourself."

She was referring to an Asian girl with dyed red hair running down to an inch of skin between the top of her white jeans and the bottom of her white dress shirt.

"Well, go hit on her already," Oxana said. "That's why we're here, isn't it?"

"Can I at least finish one drink?"

"Look what she's wearing. That girl is *begging* for somebody to spill a drink on her."

★ The letters *L, A,* and *X* pop up next to one another in all sorts of random places: at the Los Angeles airport, on lacrosse gear, on West Coast hip-hop artist The Game's third album cover, et cetera. . . .

Oxana determined that this girl and I were destined to be married. The only trouble was, my future wife was engaged in brilliant conversation with some girl wearing a ballerinian skirt (it might have been an actual tutu) and two muscular guys in formfitting shirts. One of the guys had thick leather wristbands on both wrists—black on the left and brown on the right.

Oxana and I finished our drinks and approached the foursome. I started the conversation with Wristbands—about as indirect as you could get; I didn't want my future wife to think I was on the prowl.

"My dad told me to never mix brown and black," I said to the guy, indicating his wristbands.

"What the fuck did you just say to me?"

In the man's defense, what the fuck *did* I just say to him?

"Don't be such a dick," the ballerina scolded. She turned to me and said, "He's having a shitty night. Girl stuff."

"No worries," I said. "I know how that goes. So how do you guys all know each other?"

Mystery the PUA says this question is the best way to find out whether anybody is dating anyone without directly asking.

"They work at The Bank," the ballerina said, pointing to the guys. She was referring, I assume, to the nightclub at Bellagio, not an actual bank. "And we're models," she said, pointing to herself and my bride-to-be.

Back in Chicago when a girl said, "I'm a model," she usually meant "I've got a friend who studies communications at a state college, and what he really wants to do is be a photographer, and a couple months ago he took these boring semi-nude pictures of me at his grandparents' cottage and you can see the ones he e-mailed me on my Facebook profile." But when a Las Vegas girl says that she models, she usually means that she's a promotional model. "Promotional model" is the umbrella term given to UNLV students, cocktail servers, dancers, and bartenders who, from time to time, are paid by casinos and local businesses to hold signs, hand out flyers, and give out alcohol. Promotional models also work the booths at Vegas trade shows like the Consumer Electronics Show and the Backyard Living Expo.

"What kind of modeling?" I asked.

"Artistic."

Interesting response.

"What do you two do?" the ballerina asked.

"She's a showgirl and I'm a lawy—a magician."

"Wait"—my fiancée joined the conversation. "*Who* are you two?"

"This is Rick," said Oxana, "the coolest guy in the world."

"Well, *this* year. Last year it was David Hasselhoff."

What is wrong with me? Did I take a Jay Leno pill?

"So," I said, moving on, "your ballerina friend tells me you two are models."

"I *told* you that looks like a tutu."

"It doesn't!"

"Are you tutu models? That's so adorable."

According to some PUAs, when a girl says, "I'm a model," she's trying to test you. If you get intimidated, you fail.★ PUA Ross Jeffries has a prepackaged speech that he gives in response to this sort of intimidation "test":

> I live in Los Angeles, it's where the most beautiful women in the country come to try and make it. You look around a club there, and everyone's good-looking. It makes this club room look like a dive bar. And do you know what I've learned? Beauty is common. It's something you're born with or you pay for. What counts is what you make of yourself. What counts is a great outlook and a great personality.

Here's what Kiana, my fiancée (who turned out to be Hawaiian, not Asian), had to say in response to my version of Jeffries's prepackaged speech: "So . . . are you going to ask me to dance?"

"Of course I am," I said. "Would you like to dance?"

We danced and left the club forty-five minutes later. Oxana was having fun; she didn't mind.

★ Mystery says that when a girl tells you she's a model, you should respond, "You mean a hand model?"

Here's what Kiana told me when we got outside: "It's a thousand for the whole night."

Apparently I'd picked up a hooker.

"You're kidding."

"I can do six because you're cute, but that's it."

"Shouldn't you have clarified the situation earlier?"

"Eva told you, I thought."

"The tutu girl? She said you were models—you were listening at that point."

"I thought you said you were local."

"What, is 'model' local-talk for prostitute?"

"Don't use that word."

"What, 'prostitute'? That's what—"

"If you're not interested, I'm going to go back in."

"I'm not interested."

"Fine. Four hundred."

That's quite a jump.

"Okay," I said, "you *are* joking. . . ."

"Fine. Just buy me a coffee."

"If you're being serious right now," I said, "I don't want to sleep with you."

"I figured that out. Thanks."

"I mean, not even for free."

"Are you just trying to make me feel like shit now?"

Maybe she isn't joking.

"I'm just making sure we're on the same page," I said.

"Please just buy me coffee. I need to sober up."

"What, for round two?"

"I want to sober up and go home, if that's okay with you. So hold the judgments."

"Judgments? I just told you I *personally* didn't—"

"Would you please just buy me a coffee? I don't have any money here."

I bought Kiana a coffee and she told me about her time in Vegas. She said that she used to work at an escort agency and was in the process of trying to go it alone. She told me about her regular "clients," about how much they paid her, and about how awful they were: "Disgusting in every sense of the word."

I felt bad for Kiana, but in a way, I felt even worse for her clients. This probably goes without saying, but if Kiana's clients ever heard Kiana talking about them the way she talks about them, they'd kill themselves. It wasn't just men, though. Kiana had a sour opinion of almost everything in Las Vegas. Understandably—the city had dealt her a rough hand. It does that.

Spending time with Kiana, I could already tell, would probably be disillusioning and depressing. But I wanted to do more of it. That's why I came to Vegas, after all—to befriend people like Kiana, and to learn from them.

And I did learn a big lesson from Kiana.

Of course, I had to learn it the hard way. . . .

5. You Gotta Be Honestly Sincere

In the late eighties and early nineties, Nickelodeon dominated the children's television market. I'm told that other TV stations existed at the time, but I can't remember watching them. I'm not alone—if you ever find yourself conversing with a group of twentysomethings and you don't have anything to say to them, ask them about their favorite Nickelodeon shows and it'll keep them going for hours.

On Halloween 1986, Nickelodeon presented a wonderful half-hour special, and they gave it the unfortunate title *Mystery Magical Special*. It starred *Double Dare*★ host Marc Summers and three children, one of whom was Jonathan Brandis. In the opening scene, the four are driving home from a horror movie. Due to road construction, they're forced to take a detour along a dark road.

★ *Double Dare* only ran for one season, but the show begot *Super Sloppy Double Dare,* which begot *Family Double Dare,* which begot *Celebrity Double Dare,* which begot *Super Special Double Dare,* which begot *Double Dare 2000* (which introduced the Triple Dare Challenge, the Slobstacle Course, and gooze [a fusion of goo and ooze]). So, yeah, I'd say it was *pretty* important.

Something sharp pierces one of the car's tires. The foursome stops at the nearest house, which, as Halloween luck would have it, is a spooky mansion. Hoping to find a phone to call AAA, the four let themselves in. They stumble through a secret passageway in the bookshelf, and before long the group is lost.

"We've got to find a door out of this place," Summers says.

"Well, why don't we ask him?" asks one of the children.

The kid is referring to a man standing at the other end of the room. He's wearing a tuxedo, fanning a deck of playing cards in his left hand, and twirling a single card in his right. The man is Lance Burton.★

Burton springs a deck of playing cards at a gramophone. The record spins, the needle drops, and a scratchy recording of Vivaldi's Summer Concerto plays. Burton removes the lit cigarette from his mouth and uses it to set his cane ablaze. He grabs the fire in his palm and tosses a fireball into the air. It transforms into a dove. The dove flies in a circle and back to Burton's outstretched finger. Burton takes off his purple velvet gloves and tosses them into the air. They, too, turn into

---

★ At least, it's *supposed* to be Burton. But it's not—not in that very first establishing shot. It's *Mystery Magical Special* writer/*MAGIC Magazine* editor in chief Stan Allen, with black shoe polish in his hair. Allen told me that Burton had to fly out of California before the Nickelodeon crew got every shot in, so they had to use him (Allen) as a double.

a dove. Burton manipulates scarves, candlesticks, and a newspaper, and by the time he's done virtually everything is a dove.★

When Burton is through, a severed head drops from the ceiling. The kids scream and scatter. Summers takes shelter in a phone booth, which changes him into a skeleton and then into a demonic swordsman hell-bent on slicing Burton into a million pieces. Burton grabs a fencing lance (fittingly) from the wall and the two do battle. After two minutes of tightly choreographed slashing and stabbing and jumping and ducking, Burton seeks shelter under a heavy blanket. Bad decision: The demonic swordsman plunges his weapon into the conjurer's stomach. The swordsman removes the blanket, presumably to make sure the magician is dead, and, as he does, Burton vanishes in a burst of fire, sparks, and smoke.

And then the demon swordsman removes his mask.

It's Burton.

Now this might sound silly, but that half-hour special had a profound impact on my life. I spent years trying to duplicate the swordsman illusion with my friend Steve, and then I convinced my parents to buy me a pair of

---

★ Burton performed this dove routine in Switzerland for the Fédération International des Sociétés Magiques when he was twenty-two years old. The group awarded him the Grand Prix award—the Heisman Trophy of prestidigitation. He was the youngest magician to ever win the award, and the first American.

Doves, Dagger Chest, Crystal Silk Cylinder, Ultra Die Penetration, Hippity Hop
Rabbit—my mom even sewed the playing-card-suit table cover for me.

Sacred White Doves from the Royal Tropical Fish &
Bird Haven.

Two decades later, Lance Burton is still turning gloves,
candlesticks, and sheets of newspaper into doves, only
now he does so at the Lance Burton Theatre in the
Monte Carlo Resort & Casino. Burton began his Monte
Carlo tenure in 1994, and since that time he's added
many new illusions to his repertoire. But the dove routine and the sword fight haven't changed.

Another thing that hasn't changed: Burton's persona—
that of the aw-shucks Kentucky conjurer.

"I'm well known in Kentucky," jokes Burton. "I'm the guy with the tuxedo."

Before French magician Jean Eugène Robert-Houdin—the guy from whom Houdini took his stage name—came along, magicians didn't wear tuxedos. They wore wizard outfits—the type of thing a "real" magician would wear. Robert-Houdin, though, didn't want his audience to think he was a real magician (somebody who cast spells); he wanted his audience to see him as an artist, as a man who created the illusion that he could do the impossible.★ So he dressed the same way his audience dressed when they came out to see his show: in a tuxedo.

When you consider all the deception in politics, big business, media, science, and advertising, it isn't surprising that magicians like Burton have taken to referring to themselves as "honest deceivers." Unlike dishonest mechanics who perform unnecessary repairs on your car and unethical salesmen who pitch you products they know you don't need and can't afford, Burton tells you up front he's going to trick you. He misrepresents, misdirects, and lies but does so with your implicit permission.

★ There was, however, one gig at which Robert-Houdin wanted his audience to believe he had actual magical powers. It was an assignment from Napoléon III. The Algerian Arabs were planning to rebel against the French colonizers, so Napoléon sent Robert-Houdin to Algeria to perform for the Arabs and convince them that the French had better magic—magic powerful enough to squash a potential rebellion. Robert-Houdin caught a bullet between his teeth—more on this trick later—and made an empty box so heavy that even the strongest Algerian warriors couldn't lift it. Napoléon's plan worked; Robert-Houdin broke up the mullahs.

One Friday night in the late fall, Oxana and I drove to Monte Carlo and gave Burton our implicit permission.

The curtains opened to reveal a blue translucent biomechanical humanoid form surrounded by four old-fashioned portraits. The first portrait was of Harry Kellar, the man the Masons dubbed "Greatest American Magician." Keller founded the Royal Dynasty of American Magicians and passed his title to Howard Thurston (the man in the second portrait) in 1908. Thurston passed it to Dante (number three) in the 1930s, and Dante passed it to Lee Grabel (four) in 1954. Forty years later, Grabel passed the title to Lance Burton. I know this because the recorded voice-over at the start of the show told me so, and as it did, the translucent biomechanical humanoid form in the middle burst into light and materialized into the man of the hour.

If I'd seen the illusion on television, I would have thought it was a camera trick.

Hollywood starlets are never as pretty in person, comedians aren't as funny, and action heroes aren't as tall. But Lance Burton's dove act was every bit as polished in person as it was on his *Mystery Magical Special*. It was one of those rare life occasions in which something I'd built up in my mind over the years was as impressive as I imagined it would be.

After the bird routine Burton introduced a line of show-girls, who performed a few minutes of outdated choreog-

My money's on Burton.

raphy. I got the feeling that the girls onstage knew the choreography was stale—I could tell by their smiles.

"The smile's the hardest part of the whole gig," Oxana whispered to me. "That's the note I got most often: 'Smile better.' But it's hard."★

At the end of the show Burton battled the demonic

★ English psychologist Richard Wiseman conducted an experiment to determine the difference between real smiles and fake ones. He elicited genuine smiles from subjects by making them laugh and fake smiles by asking subjects to imagine they were meeting somebody they disliked but had to be polite to. Wiseman came to the same conclusion that French scientist Guillaume Duchenne de Boulogne came to over one hundred years earlier: In a genuine smile, the muscles around the eyes tighten and pull the eyebrows down and the cheeks up, which produces tiny lines around the corners of the eyes. A fake smile produces no lines.

Wiseman's subjects got off easy—when psychologist Carney Landis wanted to study facial reactions in the 1920s, he made his subjects put their hands in buckets of water that contained live frogs. Then he *ran electricity through the buckets.* Next he handed out rats and butcher knives and *told his subjects to decapitate the rats.* If a particular subject refused, Landis decapitated a rat himself, right in front of the subject.

swordsman, for what must have been his five thousandth time.

While the dancers' choreography hadn't held up with time, the sword fight certainly had. When Burton tore off the mask and cape, the audience gasped. I could hear it.

So amidst flashy topless dance revues and breath-taking Cirque productions, there's still a role on the Las Vegas Strip for a tuxedoed honest deceiver.

"Mark was doing *Double Dare* at the time," Burton told me over the phone, "and he had this idea to do a half-hour Halloween magic show. I'm so glad that I did it, too—they ran that thing on Halloween every year, you know?"

"I *do* know," I replied. "I watched it every year. I mean, I had it on tape, too, but I still watched the actual airings, but it's not like I watched it nonstop, you know? I did lots of other stuff. . . ."

I'd initially hoped I could hide my childhood obsession from Burton for at least the first five minutes of our interview.

"The main thing I remember from that show," Burton told me, "was being tired. I was working at the Tropicana at the time. I did two shows in one night, then got on a plane and flew out, and then we began shooting early the next morning. Whenever I see the show, all I can think about is how sleepy I look."

"Well, *I* couldn't tell. I thought you looked great."

I sounded like a creepy schoolgirl. And once I realized that, I dropped my façade of journalistic detachment and told Burton about the impact the special had had on my childhood. I told him about the choreographed sword fights I attempted with my buddy Steve, and I told Burton about the doves I'd convinced my parents to buy me when I was a teenager.

"I got my first doves when I was fourteen," Burton said. "For my birthday. My mom found them through Harry Collins, who was my mentor. He was a terrific magician in Louisville, and a friend of the family. We put them in the basement with the rest of my magic stuff. I had read in magic books that you could take a refrigerator box, put some wire on it, and turn it into a cage, so that's what we did."

Next I asked Burton about his decision to wear the tuxedo. Turns out Burton started wearing a tux for the opposite reason that Robert-Houdin did—Burton wanted to stand out: "Doug Henning was very popular at the time I started wearing the tux. Doug wore the rainbow shirts and long hair, if you remember. And I looked around, and that seemed to be the popular thing to do—all the other magicians started wearing the rainbow shirts and long hair, so I thought, if everybody's going in that direction, I'll head in the opposite direction."

"And you've been wearing it ever since."

"Magicians spend way too much time thinking about costumes—*way* too much time. Sometimes I get the impression that magicians spend seventy-five percent of their time thinking about their look, trying to get jewelry to look like Criss Angel or three-piece suits to look like Penn and Teller. My recommendation to them is, spend one-half of one percent of your time thinking about your costume, and the rest of your time thinking about magic."

"Okay, here's a costume-unrelated question for you: Do you think you're more or less honest than the average person in your day-to-day life?"

"I try to be perfectly honest in everyday life. I try not to lie at all. As magicians, we practice deception, but it's an honest form of deception. If you call yourself a magician, it's implied that you're using deception. But you're doing it to amaze. Outside of magic, I don't lie, because when you lie feelings get hurt."

"But what happens when telling the truth and sparing someone's feelings come into conflict with one another?"

"You'll have to give me an example," Burton said.

"Okay, what happens when a magician friend invites you to see his show, and he's got some new trick he's been working on, and it's awful, and after the show is done he asks you what you thought?"

"I'd try to find something nice to say. I'd try to find something to compliment."

"But what if he asks you point-blank: 'What'd you think of the new trick?'"

"If you're asked point-blank like that—if somebody says, 'Gimme a straight answer,' or something like that—you've got to be honest."

When I was sixteen or seventeen, my dad loaned me his copy of Ken Uston's *Million Dollar Blackjack*. Not an attractive book—my father lost the dust jacket in the eighties, and the pages were yellowed and folded—but I didn't have much choice. My parents and I were four days into a six-day Vegas vacation, and I'd finished the books I'd brought with me. So it was either *Million Dollar Blackjack* or the book my mom was reading: *Computer Programming for People Who Like to Read Books on Computer Programming with Boring Covers and No Pictures*. Something like that.

Most people wouldn't call the highly technical *Million Dollar Blackjack* ideal pool reading, but that's where I read it: on a lounge chair by the pool, amidst hundreds of half-naked tourists, manmade rocky waterfalls, and imported palm trees.

Ken "The Wandering Jew" Uston popularized card counting in the 1970s and 1980s. *Million Dollar Blackjack* was the first major book on card-counting team play. Think *Bringing Down the House* with bushy moustaches. Years before Bill Kaplan formed the MIT team, Uston's crew took the Las Vegas casinos for hundreds of thousands—and that was back when a hundred thousand dollars meant something.

Million Dollar Blackjack isn't just about Uston's exploits. The book teaches readers how to count cards using the "Simple Plus Minus Count" system and the Uston "Advanced Point Count." In retrospect, teaching myself to count cards at The Mirage probably wasn't the smartest move. Casinos track counters using facial-recognition software that can account for age. The software converts the size and shape of a counter's eyes, nose, cheekbones, and jaw into mathematical models using algorithms with fun names like Fisherface, Eigenface, Dynamic Link Match, and the Hidden Markov Model. These models are stored in a database called the Black Book, which is managed by Griffin Investigations, Inc., the company that took down the MIT Blackjack Team. Griffin filed for bankruptcy in 2005 after losing a defamation lawsuit brought by gamblers Michael Russo and James Grosjean, who had been wrongfully arrested for cheating based on information provided to Caesars Palace by Griffin.

So maybe I'm in the clear.

I know how to count cards, but I'm not very good at it. Sometimes I win, sometimes I lose, often I break even. Still, if you tally up all the free alcohol I drink while playing blackjack, I probably come out a bit ahead, my liver a bit behind.

The night before my book reading at Borders, I went to the Gold Coast Casino. It's located about a half mile west of Bellagio, and I'd driven by it a dozen times without ever really noticing it. Owned by the Boyd

Gaming Corporation, Gold Coast caters primarily to locals and cowboys. Whereas the Bellagio features restaurants such as Michael Mina and Le Cirque, Gold Coast features T.G.I. Friday's and a restaurant called Ping Pang Pong.

It's Chinese.

My plan was to lose up to one hundred dollars, but the ATM had other plans in mind. The screen gave me these options for withdrawal:

$200	$1000
$300	$2000
$400	$3000
$500	Other

After I saw the numbers "$2000" and "$3000" on the screen, the idea of withdrawing $100 seemed insulting, to Gold Coast and to the ATM itself. Sure, there was that "Other" option, but after seeing the figures "2000" and "3000" on the screen, I understood that "Other" was strictly for addicts and hoboes.

I pressed the $200 button.

Then this screen came up:

U.S. CARDHOLDER FEE NOTICE

The owner of this ATM charges a fee of $4.99. This charge is in addition to any fees that may be assessed by your financial institution. Do you wish to continue?

As I sit here writing this sentence, $5 seems like a lot of money for an electronic transaction that probably costs a cent to process. But at the time I didn't think twice about hitting the YES button. *Well, as long as I'm taking out $200, I thought, what's another $5? Five dollars means nothing in Las Vegas. Maybe it'll buy you a handshake from a stripper, but not a firm one. Neither the handshake nor the stripper. You know what casinos call $5 chips? Nickels. They treat 'em that way, too. Las Vegans use five-dollar bills to set their hundred-dollar bills on fire.*

Long story short: I turned $200 into $300, and then I turned the $300 into a single $25 chip. I put the chip in the betting square, and the dealer, a woman with poofy eighties hair, gave me a nine and a queen. She dealt herself a ten and a six, drew another ten, and busted. She reached into her $25 chip stack and set two chips next to mine.

She was supposed to give me only one; she'd overpaid me by $25.

Then she checked her watch.

Sometimes dealers overpay players or give out money when they should be taking it. Far more often—about 75 percent of the time, based on my own observations, at least—they underpay players or take money when they should be paying it out. When I catch a dealer underpaying a player or taking his money when she should be paying him, I speak up. The player usually thanks me, and about half the time the dealer apologizes. Because most of the errors I catch are in favor of the house, it reasons that most of the errors I don't catch are in favor of the house, too. So when the dealer over-paid me by $25, I kept my mouth shut in an attempt to even things out.

I ran the $75 up to $400, counting the cards as they fell. Card counting is mostly a straightforward mathe-matical exercise, but there is a deceptive element, too. You have to make it look like you're not card count-ing. You have to socialize with the other players, drink, look around, check your watch, be obnoxious . . . as you note the value of every card that comes out of the shoe, adjust the "running count" (for multiple-deck games), adjust the level of your bet, and adjust the opti-mum play matrix accordingly.

When a blackjack shoe has lots of tens left in it, it's good for the players.★ Accordingly, counters bet big when there are lots of tens in the deck and small when most of the tens are gone. But if a counter were to bet, say, $10 when the cards were bad and $1,000 when they were good, it'd be a dead giveaway. So counters moder-ate their bet variance.

At Gold Coast, I was varying my bets between $10 and $50.

I should have smelled the trouble a mile away. All the

★ Players get more blackjacks (which pay 3:2 or 6:5), and dealers (who, unlike the players, must draw until they get 17) bust more often.

signs were there. The pit boss, a young guy in a slim suit, stared at me for ten minutes. He made a phone call, presumably to one of the guys monitoring the "eye in the sky." Then he went back to watching me. After twenty more minutes, he made a second phone call and approached me. And then it happened. In an incredibly respectful but not patronizing tone he said, "Sir, I'm afraid I'm going to have to ask that you not play any more blackjack tonight. You're just too good for us. You're welcome to play any of our other games, but you can't play blackjack. I'm sorry."

I played dumb: "You mean, because I'm winning so much?"

Laughable. I was up around $250.

"Sir"—a little less friendly now—"let's not insult each other's intelligence. Please collect your chips and cash out."

I gave him a puzzled look, collected my chips, and walked to the casino cashier to convert my "nickels" and "quarters" into actual nickels and quarters. As the woman behind the counter laid out my bills, I debated the meaning of the front of the *When the Fun Stops* gambling-addiction brochure sitting on the counter. It depicted a red sun hovering between the orange sky and the blue sea. I couldn't tell if the sun was setting (i.e., the sun in the sky represented the fun the gambler was having, but now that it's setting, her fun is coming to an end) or rising (i.e., the fun happened in the dark, and now that the sun is rising, the problem gambler has to leave the casino, go to work, face reality, et cetera).

Before I left Gold Coast I walked back to the pit boss and played dumb one last time, my thought being, a real card counter would never do such a thing; she'd get away as quickly as possible.

"I've seen the movie," I told him, referring to *21*, as if that film were my only exposure to card counting. "Did you kick me out because you thought I was counting the cards?"

"We've tracked your play for fourteen double decks," the pit boss explained. "When the count was low, you bet ten. When it was high, you bet forty and fifty. Between you and me, you're one of the most obvious counters I've seen since I started working here. I've seen guys mouth the count before—I'm telling you, I could see their lips moving from back there—but even those guys took a little while to find because of the camera angles. I got the feeling the guys upstairs kept you around for so long because they were bored."

Well, that didn't go well.

"Here's a tip," the pit boss continued. "If you're going to count, do it where there are lots of people around, lots of big bets around you."

That was it. Nothing like the movie *21*. No punches thrown, no chase through the casino with buckets of quarters flying through the air*—certainly no detour through the kitchen. So maybe my playing dumb had saved the day, after all.

But probably not—at least, not according to Jeff Ma, the MIT Blackjack Team card counter who served as the basis for the main character in the movie *21*.

"There's no point to playing dumb," Ma told me. "When they figure it out, they figure it out. The reality is they're not going to change their minds. If they've taken the time to tell you to leave, there's nothing you can do to reverse their opinion. Just politely say 'thank you' and walk away."

"So . . . given that I didn't do that, do you think my photo is being passed around the Gold Coast right now?"

"No. My guess would be no. At Gold Coast, for fifty-dollar bets, they're probably not going to bother putting you in the Black Book or talking to the Agency. I've never been in Gold Coast, so I don't know how they handle action there, but it's such a small amount of money, I can't believe anyone would really care."

---

* Nobody carries buckets of quarters around Vegas casinos anymore. Players feed dollars directly into slot machines, which print out tickets showing how much they've won or lost (assuming they haven't lost everything, in which case they don't even get a ticket). The casinos figured out that players wasted valuable time plunking coins into machines one at a time—time that could be spent pushing the MAX BET button. Most casinos phased out quarter slots over the past decade and phased in ticketed penny slots. Penny slots sound like the perfect game to play in a sagging economy, but they're not. Some machines require you to bet at least forty pennies per spin, and up to sixteen hundred. Most penny machines allow you to bet at least a couple dollars per spin. In 2007, Nevada casinos raked in over 160 billion pennies from penny slot players.

"But if nobody cares about that kind of action," I said, "how did I get caught so quickly?"

"You were playing double deck. In general, there's more scrutiny in those games—single and double deck. So I guess it doesn't surprise me that they tracked you through fourteen decks. But it sounds like the main flaw in what you did is where you went."★

"So I shouldn't go back. . . ."

"My guess is that if you went back and if you got caught, they'd be a little bit meaner to you. They might try to backroom you or get you to sign trespassing papers."

"And . . . that's it?"

"What do you mean?" Ma asked.

"I mean, I wouldn't get beat up?"

"No, you're fine."

"So the media exaggerates the bad things that happen to counters. . . ."

"No and yes. The stories are simplified. It's simple to say, 'If you count cards you'll get beat up.' That's what the movies and the media has portrayed. On the one hand, that's not what usually happens; on the other hand, casinos can actually do worse stuff. In the Bahamas, we had a couple thrown in jail for a weekend, and they took back the money. It was so traumatic for them that they ended

---

★ Card-counting expert Richard Marcus confirmed this much: "Gold Coast has always been one of the rankest casinos in Vegas," he told me. "To kick you out over a ten-to-fifty-dollar spread is really pathetic."

up getting a divorce. And in Shreveport, some guys followed us off a riverboat and followed us in a truck with a gun rack. That wasn't the first time we'd been threatened with a gun, either. But mostly the intimidation is psychological, not physical."

"Still doesn't sound pleasant."

"It wasn't. But remember, this all happened ten years ago. I don't know whether things have gotten better since then. But the biggest problem for us is that a lot of casino security people don't understand the difference between counting and cheating. They think of card counters as cheaters. I don't think a lot of people doing these menacing things even realize the difference. There was one time when security was kicking me out of Rio and they were trying to backroom me, take my picture, and I told them, 'If you don't want my action, I'll leave,' and the security guard was like, 'No, you have to come with us,' and his boss had to step in and say, 'No, he doesn't.'"

"That doesn't sound so bad."

"It shouldn't be. Counters shouldn't matter so much to casinos. Think about the MIT team. We were one of the most capitalized teams in history, and in our best year—*best* year—we probably won a million or just over a million. The Greeks, Tommy Hyland's team— let's say they took in a couple million each, too. Let's say we took twenty million together. Well, spread that out over twenty or thirty casinos, and then factor in all the people who try to count but can't (and lose lots of money in the process). We're not talking about much money here—relatively, I mean."

Yes, relatively, I thought, as I imagined all the things I could do with that much cash.

"How do you go from dealing with these huge sums to living a normal life?" I asked.

"That's a real issue. My blackjack days gave me a perverted sense of money and relative value of money. When you've gambled hundreds of thousands of dollars, making a hundred-dollar bet is nothing. But in reality, there's a lot you can do with a hundred dollars."

The Town Square shopping center on Las Vegas Boulevard is one of those impossibly clean strip malls with speakers built into the cement. Less strip mall, more Main Street, USA, really. About twenty people assembled in Town Square's Borders café to drink coffee, gingerbread lattes, gingerbread mochas—Seattle's Best was really pushing the gingerbread drinks at the time—and to hear me talk about my previous book, *Lawyer Boy*. I discussed the book and law school, and then answered questions about my path to publication. Then I performed a magic trick I'd thought up earlier that day.

"I'm going to show you something I learned right

after moving to Vegas.* It's not a magic trick so much as it's a gambling move that you could use to cheat your friends.† You couldn't do this in a casino, but you could do it in a private poker game where the deal passes around the table.‡"

I unwrapped a new deck of Bicycle cards and spread them across the café table. I called three people from the audience up to the table and asked each of them to shuffle the cards.

"Make sure the audience can see the cards at all times," I instructed my volunteers. "Don't even step in front of the cards as you walk back to your seat."

I stood far off to the side so there'd be no way I could manipulate the deck.

"I'm going to demonstrate for you what card cheats call an 'invisible deck switch.' I'm going to switch this deck of shuffled cards for an unshuffled deck right before your eyes. And even though you know exactly what to look for, you're not going to see it happen."

I removed my suit jacket and pulled back my sleeves.

"Whatever you do, don't take your eyes off the cards."

When the third volunteer finished shuffling, I took the cards back with my outstretched hand and set them back on a café table, facedown. I stepped away from the

_____

* Not true.
† Also not true, just a magic trick.
‡ Ditto.

table, snapped my fingers, returned to the table, turned the cards face up, and spread them across the surface. Every card was in order (e.g., ace of hearts, two of hearts, three of hearts, et cetera).

Okay, now I'm going to tell you how I did it.

I feel comfortable sharing this trick's secret with you because I invented it and I don't foresee anybody else performing it any time soon. Magicians' code★ forbids me from revealing another magician's trick to you, but I think I have some leeway with my own conjuring creations. So here goes: I didn't actually switch the deck. I know how to do a deck switch, but I couldn't get away with doing one after telling an audience, "Watch out for a deck switch." No magician could.

The real secret was in the "volunteers." They were professional magicians from Darwin's magic club, who told me they'd be coming to the reading. I told them to play dumb and to false shuffle the cards† when I called them to assist me.

Of course, I didn't reveal all that to the audience, so I wasn't surprised when somebody in the back shouted, "How'd you do it?" What surprised me was who was doing the shouting. It was Zella the bartender. She must have come in at the very end.

★ An informal collection of professional advice, like "Never repeat a trick," and, "Don't perform a trick without sufficient practice," and, "Wear leather pants," and "Don't fasten the top four buttons of your shirt."
† A false shuffle looks like a regular shuffle but keeps all the cards in order.

"If I told you," I said, "I'd have to kill you."★

"Tell me!"

"Buy me a coffee and I'll see what I can do."

"I'll get you a water," Zella replied. "It's free here."

Cute.

The reading was pretty much over at that point. Everybody except Zella left, including Oxana, who was definitely trying to set us up. Zella and I left Borders and strolled around Town Square.

"That guy behind the bar at JET," I said, "wearing the suit—your manager, right?"

"Right, that's Austin."

"Sounds like he's pretty strict," I said. "You mentioned him being upset with you. . . ."

"I gave two drinks to my friend Craig, who was visiting from Arizona. And Austin got pissed."

"Doesn't seem like it'd be that big of a deal."

"Austin just doesn't like Craig. We went out to Stoney's a couple nights before that night, and Austin didn't like him then."

"Is Austin interested in you?"

"You mean interested in dating me?"

"Yeah."

"Why do you ask?"

"He might see Craig as a threat. . . ."

★ Standard magician response. Other standards include, "I can't tell you. They'll take away my union card," and, "Very well, thank you." Hardy har har.

"Yeah, Austin might be interested."

"Might?"

"After I split up with my ex—the one Oxana apparently told you about, which I can't believe, by the way—Austin asked me out. And I turned him down, but it was awkward because he's not just my boss at JET; he gets me other gigs, too, and I need the money right now."

"I do modeling for him sometimes. I mean, not *for* him. He books me, I mean. He opened a model agency; well, he's *in the process* of opening a model agency, and— Don't look at me like that—like you don't believe me. . . ."

"Just sounds kind of sketchy is all."

"That's how I met Oxana—on a gig he booked me. People start modeling agencies all the time here. And girls belong to lots of them. You don't have to sign an exclusive agreement or anything like that. Nevada is a right-to-work state."

Maybe Zella's right. Maybe it's not as sketchy as it sounds. Maybe I'm just being paranoid because of the whole Elena situation—the one that pushed me over the edge and to Vegas in the first place.

Then again, Elena had accused me of being overly paranoid, too. . . .

"I can't work these bartending and modeling jobs forever. I realize that. Unlike a lot of the girls here. But while I can get those jobs, I've got to take them. I'm under a mountain of debt: student loans, family slash medical stuff—but that's a story for another day."

I frowned.

"Don't be sad," Zella said. "Give me a year or two to get all that stuff paid off, and then I can be your sugar mama . . . long as you give me a hot plate to come home to."

"Does the hot plate have to have food on it?"

"You can't just run the dish through the dishwasher, if that's what you mean."

We rode the escalator up to Blue Martini and drank a couple half-price cocktails (half price because Zella was industry). We discussed school (Zella studied economics and marketing), religion (she alternates between Catholicism and agnosticism), and the bisexual escort she used to date. She, too, told me that they'd always used protection—she, like Oxana, really emphasized that—and from that I deduced that she might be interested in sleeping with me.

We ended the night with a kiss.

6. Control and the Illusion of It

The Aladdin Casino opened in 1966, reopened in 1976, closed in 1997, imploded in 1998, re-reopened in 2000, reclosed shortly after, and re-re-reopened in 2007 as Planet Hollywood Resort & Casino. Planet Hollywood went after the younger Palms/Hard Rock demographic with its lingerie-clad blackjack dealers, Miracle Mile shopping mall, and Irish hypnomagician Keith Barry.

A magician might seem like an odd choice for the younger demographic. The only thing most twenty-somethings like about magicians is making fun of them. And truth be told, most magicians make easy targets. But Keith Barry is a genuinely cool guy (i.e., not just cool because he's European), so he's a good fit. Oxana and I saw him on *The Ellen DeGeneres Show* one afternoon, and then we got tickets to see his show.

On the way to Planet Hollywood, Oxana said, "This guy better not call me onstage. I don't want to take my top off tonight."

"He's not one of *those* hypnotists," I assured her.

I meant that Barry wasn't X-rated like Anthony Cools at Paris (who gets his inductees to act like they're auditioning for a porn film) or Michael Johns and Terry Stokes (who get their inductees to act as though they're doing infomercials for vibrators).

We left my mom's SUV in the Harley-Davidson Café parking structure, right under the *HARLEY-DAVIDSON CAFÉ CUSTOMERS ONLY/ALL OTHERS WILL BE TOWED* sign, which Oxana assured me was sarcastic.

Barry takes over Planet Hollywood's second-floor Stomp Out Loud theater after the Stomp crew hangs up its metal trash cans and wooden brooms for the night. He took the stage wearing tight blue jeans with thick white stitching and a military-style blazer over a graphic tee. He asked the single ladies in the audience to stand up, and thirty or forty women, including Oxana, did so. Barry pointed in Oxana's direction and said, "You in the busy top—could you join me onstage?"

Oxana was wearing a leopard print blouse; he was pointing at her.

"I fucking knew it," she muttered under her breath. "Every time. Every fucking time."

She plastered on her showgirl smile and joined Barry onstage.

"Your name?"

"Oxana."

"Oxana—lovely. Please stand right next to me as I

ask all the single ladies in the audience to sit down and the single men to stand up."

We did.

"Now Oxana, I'd like you to choose one of these gentlemen—somebody you'd like to make a deep connection with."

I was afraid she'd cop out and pick me, but she pointed to a guy in the back. When he got on the stage it became clear he was half her age . . . and half her height.

"Interesting choice," Barry commented. "Now, I'd like you two to place your hands on each other's shoulders."

They did.

"And rock back and forth, in unison. Back and forth and back and forth."

Back and forth they rocked.

"Stare into each other's eyes. And now imagine each other slathered in baby oil."

I could tell from her facial expression that Oxana didn't like where that was going . . . but, it turned out, it wasn't going anywhere.

"Okay, enough of that," Barry said, much to Oxana's relief.

The hypnomagician instructed Oxana and her new guy to sit on matching wooden foldout chairs positioned about fifteen feet apart.

"I'm going to ask you both to close your eyes," he told them.

And they did.

He told Oxana, "I want you to be aware of all the different sensations around you. We're going to try a voodoo experiment right now. Don't say anything and don't open your eyes until I tell you to."

Oxana closed her eyes.

Barry walked behind the guy and touched him on the back twice.

"Oxana, did you feel anything?" Barry asked.

"Yes," she replied.

"What did you feel?"

"A touch."

"Just one?"

"No, two touches."

"And where did you feel the touches?"

"On my back."

He hadn't gone anywhere near her.

He repeated the demonstration, this time touching the guy four times on his arm.

"Did you feel anything, Oxana?"

"Yes—four touches."

"Where?"

"On my left arm."

The audience applauded and Barry encouraged the two to swap phone numbers. The guy looked more interested in the exchange than Oxana did.

Several illusions later, Barry said, "If you're a strong guy, stand up right now so I can see you."

Magicians ask for "strong guys" when they need assistants to pound on boxes to check for trapdoors or to tie them up for escape demonstrations. I stood up and volunteered, feeling confident that if I were called on, it would not be for a hypnotism bit. After all, a stage hypnotist selects hypnotic inductees in stages. First he gives a "compliance test" to the entire audience. For example, he might say, "Everybody stand up, and follow my instructions. I want you to feel your arms getting very heavy. Heavier and heavier. In a minute I'm going to ask you to lift your arms, but you won't be able to because they are so heavy. Okay, go ahead and lift your arms." Then the hypnotist will call to the stage the people whose arms are still at their sides. He'll give that preselected group another, more complex compliance test and pick the three or four most susceptible subjects to remain onstage with him for a more complex hypnosis demonstration. Hypnotists don't want to risk calling on somebody who, like me, can't or doesn't want to be hypnotized.

The ability to be hypnotized, I'm told, requires a level of trust only found in people who haven't dated the girls I've dated. It also requires the ability to surrender control completely, whereas my specialty has always been the inability to relinquish even the slightest bit of control, even in situations in which it'd be to my advantage to do so.

"You, sir."

Barrry pointed right at me.

When I got onstage, Barry's exact words, I believe, were these: "Tonight you're going to be hypnotized."

Fuck.

Barry sat me on one of the wooden chairs and waved his fingers before my eyes.

"What's your name?"

"Rick."

"Everybody say, 'Hi, Rick!'"

"*Hi, Rick!*" shouted the audience.

"Say, 'Bye, Rick!'"

"*Bye, Rick!*"

Barry yanked my arm and I flopped over in my chair.

"Sleep. Breathe in through your nose and out through your mouth, and drift off to sleep and listen to the sound of my voice. Listen to the sound of my voice very carefully. I want you to imagine that you're going on a vacation to the Bahamas. I want you to imagine yourself lying on a chaise lounge, on the beach, maybe reading a book."

Well, that's odd, I thought. *I am going on a vacation to the Bahamas with my parents. And I do plan to lie on a lounge chair and read a book while I'm there.*

Just a coincidence, I told myself. *This isn't real. This isn't happening.*

"I want you to imagine a girl in the distance. A brunette girl, wearing a bikini, maybe smiling at you."

I must have smiled back, because the audience started to laugh.

"And now imagine she's right in front of you, Rick. And open your eyes."

I did, and there she was. Standing right in front of me. Wearing a red and white polka-dot bikini.

So maybe I can be hypnotized, after all.

Or maybe not. It took me a second, but I gathered that the girl wasn't really a figment of my imagination. She must have walked out onstage after I closed my eyes. The audience laughed because they realized Barry would soon have me open my eyes and discover her.

"Rick, put your hands underneath Stephanie's armpits and lift her straight up."

I did—no sweat.

"Good. I want you to imagine right now that she weighs five hundred pounds and you will not be able to lift her. You will not be able to lift her. She weighs five hundred pounds. Okay, try and lift her now."

Stephanie wouldn't budge. It felt like she'd put on four hundred pounds in ten seconds.

"Good. Take a seat, Rick, and close your eyes again. Let's try something a little different now. I'm going to take away your motor skills . . . right *now*. Feel your motor skills slipping away. Motor skills slipping away, Rick. Good, now, when I snap my fingers, I want you to open your eyes, and your motor skills will be gone."

Barry snapped his fingers and I opened my eyes again.

"How do you feel?" he asked.

"Fine."

"Stand up and walk over here."

I complied.

Barry took a pair of scissors from the table and used them to cut several strips off a piece of paper. He handed me the scissors and paper and instructed me to do the same.

I couldn't get the scissors open. It felt as though they'd been locked shut. I tried using two hands to separate the blades, but that didn't work, either.

Barry took the scissors back and opened them easily.

"I've done the first part for you," he said. "Now you just close 'em on the paper."

I couldn't do that, either, much to the audience's delight.

"One last thing, Rick. I need you to sit down and close your eyes for me one more time. Good. Now listen carefully, from the time you wake up to the time that you walk out of the theater today, if you hear me snap my fingers, I want you to shout, *'Barry, I'm a bloody leprechaun! Where's me pot of gold?!'* Jump right out of your seat and scream, at the top of your lungs, *'Barry, I'm a bloody leprechaun! Where's me pot of gold?!'* Okay, in three seconds, you're going to wake up and you're going to feel refreshed, like you just woke up from a long, rejuvenating nap. Three. Two. One. Awake!"

I left the stage and returned to my seat. Throughout the next hour Barry performed some impressive demonstrations. I can't recall all their specifics, though, because my attention was focused on his right-hand fingers. I was waiting for them to snap.

But the snap never came, and I began to worry I'd made up the whole thing in my mind. I began to worry that I didn't remember what exactly transpired onstage. I began to worry that Barry hadn't actually told me to pretend to be a leprechaun. I began to think about how it'd look from the audience's point of view if I were to stand up and demand a pot of gold for no apparent reason. *Hasn't that diva gotten enough stage time already?* they'd say. I have similar thoughts every day. If I'm at a dinner party, for example, I'll think to myself, *What's the most embarrassing thing I could say right now, and what would I do if I accidentally said it?*

Barry picked up a lightbulb and said, "I need extreme silence for this. This is very, very difficult. In a second I'm going to snap my fingers, and when I do, I want all of you to focus your energy on the lightbulb."

I whispered to Oxana, "When I was onstage, did he tell me to pretend to be a leprechaun when—"

Barry snapped and I took the plunge. I sprang from my seat and, in full Irish accent, cried, *"Barry! I'm a leprechaun! Where's me pot of gold?!"*

The audience went silent. It was probably just a fraction of a second, but it felt like a minute. Then the silence turned into laughter, and I put my hand over my mouth—the universal signal for *I can't believe what I just said.*

"You'll get it after the show," Barry said, in the tone you use when you're talking a person out of jumping off a building ledge. And then he shattered the lightbulb with his mind.

So, was I really hypnotized? Is hypnotism even real?

The answer to that second question might depend on how you define "hypnotism."★

One guy who hangs out at Gary Darwin's magic club defined hypnosis for me as "a state of heightened suggestibility." If that's how you define hypnosis, then yes, hypnotism definitely exists. But by defining hypnosis as "a state of heightened suggestibility" you risk defining it out of existence. I've heard several hypnotists give variations on this speech: "Do you ever find yourself driving on the freeway, maybe at night, and listening to your favorite song on the radio, and after a couple minutes, you look up and see that you've missed your exit? Well, *that's hypnosis*. You were hypnotized by the rhythm of the road." I've even heard one hypnotist say,

---

★ Here's how the Executive Committee of the American Psychological Association, Division of Psychological Hypnosis, defines it:

Hypnosis typically involves an introduction to the procedure during which the subject is told that suggestions for imaginative experiences will be presented. The hypnotic induction is an extended initial suggestion for using one's imagination, and may contain further elaborations of the introduction. A hypnotic procedure is used to encourage and evaluate responses to suggestions. When using hypnosis, one person (the subject) is guided by another (the hypnotist) to respond to suggestions for changes in subjective experience, alterations in perception, sensation, emotion, thought or behavior. . . . If the subject responds to hypnotic suggestions, it is generally inferred that hypnosis has been induced.

"You know that feeling you get when you sink into a warm bathtub and you're just completely relaxed and you can sense every part of your body? That state that you're in—*that's a hypnotic trance state.*"

Of course, most people understand stage hypnotism to be something more specific. Most people understand stage hypnotism to be the process by which a hypnotist brings subjects into a mental state in which the subjects are not fully conscious and are susceptible to suggestion—so much so that they'll do things they wouldn't otherwise do.

It's difficult to prove that *that* kind of hypnosis exists, because everything that occurs during hypnotism performances can be explained by non-hypnotic phenomena, like peer pressure and the desire to please. Remember, a lot of hypnotism participants *enjoy* being the center of attention. They enjoy doing outlandish things before groups of people—and that's why the hypnotists selected them to participate. And even some typically shy subjects relish the excuse to release their inhibitions in a controlled forum.

Those are some of the reasons that magician/mentalist Amazing Kreskin cut the hypnosis portion from his act. Kreskin now rallies against stage hypnotism, saying this:

> For nineteen years I had believed in . . . the sleep-like hypnotic trance, practicing it constantly.

Though I had nagging doubts at times, I wanted to believe in it. There was an overpowering mystique about putting someone to sleep—something that set me and all other hypnotists apart. We were marvelous Svengalis or Dr. Mesmers, engaged in a supernatural practice of sorts. Then it all collapsed—for me anyway.

Kreskin and other hypnotism skeptics say that many stage hypnotists whisper to their onstage audience participants things like, "When I tell you to do something, just do it. It'll be our secret. Have fun with it. Let's put on a really good show together." The skeptics say that other hypnotists use stooges—actors who pretend to be hypnotized.

I can't tell you what percent of stage hypnotists use tricks like these, but I can tell you that Keith Barry did not whisper anything to me when I was onstage. He didn't have any of his assistants whisper anything to me, either. And I was definitely not a stooge.

But was I hypnotized?

Well, I was fully cognizant of everything that went on during my "hypnotic state" and I didn't feel any different throughout the performance.* So I don't think I was hypnotized in the narrow sense of the word. But I

---

* It's technically possible that Barry hypnotized me in such a way that I felt as though I was not being hypnotized.

was probably hypnotized in the broadest sense of the word, in that (1) Barry told me to act like a leprechaun, (2) I did act like a leprechaun, and (3) acting like a leprechaun is not something I'd usually do.

But I can explain why I did it, and my explanation doesn't involve what is commonly understood as "hypnosis": I didn't want to let Barry down. Simple as that. I threw my hands over my mouth after asking Barry for the gold because I wanted to put on a good show.

Of course, my experience onstage doesn't prove that hypnosis (in the narrow sense) *doesn't* exist. It doesn't suggest that hypnosis is fake any more than it suggests that I have trust issues. (Remember, most hypnotists cede that you can't be hypnotized unless you want to be hypnotized.) It's hard to prove the existence of hypnosis, but it's impossible to fully disprove its existence.★

At the end of the show, Barry moved out of hypnotist mode and back into magician mode. He tossed a giant Frisbee to the crowd and invited the man who caught it onto the stage to participate in the second most dangerous trick in all of magic:† Spike. When a magician flubs

---

★ And what about the scissors (which I really couldn't operate) and the girl (whom I really couldn't lift)? Well, let's just say Barry blends hypnosis with magic in such a way that it's hard to say where the magic tricks end and where the hypnosis begins. But regardless of method—and this is what's most important—Barry performs a baffling act.

† The most dangerous trick in all of magic is the bullet catch. Penn & Teller perform this trick nightly at the Rio, and they've been doing it for a while. Other magicians haven't had so much luck. The bullet catch killed English magician Kia Khan Khruse in 1818. Two years later, German magician De Linsky killed his wife performing the trick. Six years later, a performer named De Grisy

Spike, nobody dies; they just get maimed—that's why it doesn't qualify as magic's most dangerous trick. The thing that makes Spike so dangerous is the frequency with which magicians mess it up. About two dozen magicians have flubbed the bullet catch in the past two hundred years; based on my informal research, about the same number have flubbed Spike in the past decade.

Barry set four wooden coasters on the table. One of them had a four-inch metal spike attached to it. He demonstrated the spike's sharpness by pounding it on the table. He blindfolded himself and then asked the volunteer to place four paper cones over the coasters. Then Barry held a towel in front of the covered coasters and instructed the volunteer to mix them up, so now nobody (except for the volunteer) knew where the spike was. Next Barry put the blindfold on the spectator and mixed the covered coasters up himself, so not even the volunteer knew where the spike was. And then Barry

---

killed his son; then Dr. Epstein, then deLine, then Michael Hatal, then Bosco Blumenfeld, then Edvin Lindberg, and then Chung Ling Soo were also killed. There are all sorts of ways the bullet catch can go wrong. Here are two examples:

Dr. Epstein used a magic wand as a ramrod. One night, part of his wand broke off in the gun, and when the trigger was pulled the wand tip flew at the magician like a bullet.

Magician Chung Ling Soo (real name: William Robinson) used a trick gun that took real bullets but didn't fire them. The gun was rigged in such a way that the loaded bullets dropped from the chamber to the base. Problem was, over the years, the gun's secret passage had become clogged with unburned gunpowder residue. One night, the buildup prevented the bullet from dropping properly and the fake gun fired like a real one. Upon being shot in the chest, Chung Ling Soo said, "Lower the curtain." It was the first time he'd ever broken character (by speaking English) onstage.

put the blindfold back on himself and had the spectator mix the coasters up one last time.

Barry asked the spectator for his hand, and the man gave it without hesitation. Strong evidence that this guy had no idea of what was about to happen.

Barry, still blindfolded, held the spectator's hand directly above the cones.

"Move your hand above one of them."

The spectator moved his hand above the cone on the left.

"Do you think the spike is under here?" Barry asked.

"No?" the spectator guessed.

Barry slammed the man's other hand down on the cone, which folded like an accordion.

You can find this picture of Keith Barry performing his "spike" illusion in the dictionary under *schadenfreude*.

"Jesus Christ!" the spectator shouted.

"Good decision," said Barry. "Hold your hand above another cone."

The spectator realized that Barry was going to slam his hand down on whichever one he picked. The spectator realized (sorry in advance, but here it comes) that his fate was in his own hands.

"Another cone," said Barry. "You're in control of this."

"I don't want to be in control."

"Just do it. Move your hand."

The guy winced and moved his hand to the cone next to the crushed one. He grimaced and turned his head away.

"Do you think the spike is under here?" Barry asked.

"No?" the guy said.

Barry slammed down the guy's hand.

Another miss.

"Good decision," said Barry. "Now pick one last cone."

He picked the one on the right.

"You don't think the spike is under here?" Barry asked.

"I don't know."

"What does your intuition tell you?"

"I don't . . . please."

"You're in control of this. Tell me. Is the spike under here?"

"I don't know!"

"Yes or no?!"

"No!"

Barry slammed the guy's hand down.

No spike, no blood. Just relief.

Most of the relief belonged to the guy onstage, but some of it belonged to me as well. Unlike most people in the audience, I knew that this illusion was *actually* dangerous—that magicians *really do* mess it up from time to time. I've seen videos of magicians messing it up, and it's horrific. I've seen a video of Menny Lindenfeld slamming his own hand into a propped-up butcher knife. I've seen him shake the blood off his hand and onto his spectator's face. I've seen another video of a magician (with a blurred-out face) slamming some poor woman's hand onto a Styrofoam cup that had a giant spike underneath. I've heard the woman scream. And you know what the magician said to the audience? "Sometimes magic goes wrong." Then he said, "Thanks very much," and he bowed, and the audience applauded.

What if I'd caught Barry's Frisbee? I wondered. And then I shuddered.

I found Barry in the theater lobby after the show and asked him about the origins of Spike.

"I invented the method, but nobody knows exactly how I do it. People try to figure it out, but they always get the method wrong and that's why so many people have messed it up."

"Would you ever assist another magician with the trick?"

"Absolutely not, and let me tell you why: When I do a trick, I'm in control. When somebody else does the trick, they're in control. If I'm onstage for a dangerous trick—anything with spikes or blades or saws or guns—I want to be the one in control. That way, if something goes wrong, I'll have no one to blame but myself."

On the way to the car, I asked Oxana what she would have done if she had caught the Frisbee.

"Gone onstage," she said.

"I mean, would you have stayed there when you learned what the magic trick was about?"

"Yeah."

"You wouldn't have been scared?" I asked.

"I'd be scared, but I wouldn't run offstage or do anything like that."

"But what if he messed up and slammed your hand down?"

"He wouldn't do that," Oxana said.

"But what if he did?"

"What?" Oxana said. "You're saying you would have run offstage?"

"Maybe," I replied.

"Wow, Rick, you've really got some trust issues, don't you?"

Maybe.

7. The Hard Way to Make an Easy
Twenty-three Hundred Dollars

Y ou're never coming home!"
It was my mom. She'd been calling almost every day, asking me trick questions like, "Do you ever plan to come back?" and, "What did I ever do to you?" and, "What are you trying to prove?" and, "Is this some sort of protest against me?" I assured her that I was planning to return to the Midwest, that she didn't do anything wrong, that I wasn't trying to prove anything to anyone, and that I wasn't protesting her parenting skills or those of my father.

But she didn't believe me.

"You said you'd be gone for a few weeks."

"I miscalculated," I said.

"Some miscalculation! You've been in Vegas for four months."

"I'm bad at math."

"Don't tell me you're bad at math. You got seven hundred something on the SAT math section."

"I got lucky."

"That's bologna. Do you want me to pull out your old report cards and read you your math grades?"

"Please don't," I pleaded.

She'd do it.

"Then tell me why you're still in Las Vegas."

What could I tell her? That I couldn't come back to the Midwest because I was too busy getting kicked out of casinos, meeting working girls, and pretending to be a leprechaun?

Luckily I didn't have to tell her anything:

"Hang on. I'm getting another call," I said.

"I can hear that."

"I'll call you back tomorrow."

"Be careful out—"

I clicked over to Zella.

"What's the plan for tonight?" she wanted to know.

We'd gone out a couple times since our impromptu Town Square date. The first time we invited Oxana to be our chaperone, and the other times it was just us two. Zella seemed to really like me, but judging from what she told me about her ex-boyfriends, she also seemed to have really bad taste in men. I was careful not to discuss her most recent ex or the breakup. *She'll mention it if she wants to talk about it,* I figured. *She probably just wants to forget about it.* We talked a lot about her and Austin. About what a strange, demanding guy he was. And the more she told me about him, the more worried I got.

"Let's meet on the Strip and figure things out from there," I suggested.

"The Strip? Really?"

Locals view the Strip the way Kissimmites view the Magic Kingdom: as a cubicle farm. Still, I persuaded Zella to join me at Bellagio for a drink. We met at the floor-to-ceiling chocolate fountain behind the botanical gardens and walked to the bar at Sensi.

When we arrived I ordered us wine, and right after I did Geoffrey Fieger sat down next to me.

Midwestern trial attorney Geoffrey Fieger defended Dr. Jack Kevorkian (aka Dr. Death) and represented the family of Scott Amedure in the *Jenny Jones Show* trial.* In the past thirty years he's won more multimillion-dollar verdicts than any other lawyer in the country. He's pretty famous in Michigan.

"Zella, this is Geoffrey. Geoffrey: Zella."

That was a fair introduction in that it left both parties equally confused. Fieger had no idea who the hell I was—let alone Zella—and Zella certainly wasn't expecting a second guest. I turned to Zella and gave her a look that was meant to convey, *Be on your best behavior; this guy might get me a job one day,* but it must have come off as a *play along* look, because Zella said to Fieger, "Rick's told me so much about you!"

---

*Amedure's friend killed him after Amedure revealed his homosexual crush.

She must have assumed that Fieger was a good friend of mine, that I'd told him all about her but had somehow forgotten to tell her about him (what a close friend he was, what a great guy he was, et cetera). Luckily for me, Fieger's ego is as grand as his talent, so he didn't give a second thought to the "told me so much about you" line.

"Zella's a bartender at JET," I said.

"I figured you were a model."

"I like your friend," Zella said.

Before Fieger had a chance to question our "friendship," I asked him what he wanted to drink.

"Wine is good. Just a glass, though. Then I'm off to bed. I'm still on Michigan time and my jet's flying out at six tomorrow."

Zella arched her eyebrows the way you do when somebody says "my jet" in passing.

"So what'd you think of the speech?" Fieger asked.

Moment of truth: I could tell him I thought it was pretty good and change the topic, or I could go for the more honest, "What speech?" approach.

I chose the latter.

"You're not with the convention?" Fieger asked.

"No."

"Who are you?"

"Rick Lax."

"Why does your name sound familiar to me?"

"I wrote a book about law school."

"*Lawyer Boy*? That's you?"

Let me explain how awesome that moment was. Fieger had heard of my book, I presume, because I had contacted his assistant a couple months earlier and asked her to ask him for a jacket blurb. But Zella didn't know that—she just knew that some guy with a private jet apparently knew who I was.

Like I said, famous and modest.

"So the speech . . . ?" Zella asked.

"I was speaking to a plaintiffs organization called Mass Torts Made Perfect—me and Fred Thompson and Bill Maher."

"What was your speech about?" I asked.

"Me," Fieger replied.

"Fieger is an expert on himself," I explained.

"Well, you seem to know a lot about me," said Fieger, "but what about you two? How long have you two been going out?"

"Four," I said.

"Months? Years?"

"Dates."

"You're lying," Fieger said. You're probably engaged—I can tell."

Most people might feel uncomfortable telling a stranger, "You're lying," but trial lawyers do this all the time. Plus, Fieger might have been being facetious.

"You know," Zella said, "lying is a sin."

Speaking of facetious . . .

"And, what, you never sin?" Fieger asked.

"Of course not. Sinners go to hell. Dogs, medicine men, fornicators, murderers, idolaters, and *everyone of false light and false speech*. But don't take my word for it, check out Revelations Twenty-two Fifteen."

Okay, maybe she's not being facetious.

"Do you have the whole Bible memorized?" Fieger asked.

"Actually, yes."

Our jaws dropped.

"Kidding," Zella said. "I just know some quotes on the big topics: lying, sex, faith, death—but that's about it."

"So *you* lie, too," Fieger pointed out.

"It was a joke."

"Well, where do you draw the line?" Fieger asked, transitioning into cross.

I'm telling you, lawyers do that. Date one and find out for yourself.

Zella's phone rang and she answered. As Fieger and I continued our conversation, we overheard all sorts of "yesses" and "uh-huhs" on Zella's end of the line.

"It's Austin," said Zella. "He says I have to meet him at Mandalay."

"At eleven o'clock on Friday night?" Fieger asked. "I thought Rick said you worked at JET."

"This is a modeling thing."

"You're an on-call model?"

"No, it's not a gig; he's meeting with a prospective client."

"And you have to be there for it?" Fieger asked.

"That does seem odd," I added, as if I knew anything about the modeling industry.

"Pretty standard," Zella said.

"Hmm," I replied.

"You're being paranoid again. It's fine."

Every day Zella's situation was reminding me more and more of Elena's, and I didn't like it one bit.

One Wednesday in winter—how cute is it that Las Vegans still call it winter?—Gary Darwin brought another special guest to Boomers: John Calvert. Calvert performed from 10:00 P.M. to 1:00 A.M. and the audience of magicians sat captivated the whole time. Calvert produced cigarettes from his fingertips, broke and restored a spectator's watch, and escaped from tightly tied ropes in seconds.

John Calvert was ninety-seven years old.

"I invited him to come when he was a hundred," Darwin told me before the elderly conjurer took the stage, "but he's booked solid."★

At one point in the show, the back legs of Calvert's chair slid off the back of a six-inch raised platform. The chair tipped backward and Calvert tipped with it. A couple of the guys rushed the stage, but Calvert waved

---

★ You can catch him at the London Palladium theater on his one hundredth birthday, August 5, 2011.

them off and insisted on getting up himself. He must have landed on something sharp, because his left hand was covered in blood. He soaked up the blood with a couple of bar napkins and said, "A thing like this shouldn't stop you from performing."

And then he continued on as if nothing had happened.

"For my last effect," Calvert said, "I need the help of somebody who isn't afraid of the devil."

His assistants removed the white blanket covering the big prop that had been sitting in the back corner of the room for the duration of the show, a long table with a giant buzz saw on the end. It was the scariest magic prop I'd ever seen. Not because it was the biggest or the sharpest . . . but because it looked like the saw blade could fall off at any minute.

"My brother made this for me out of parts left over from World War Two operating tables," Calvert said.

Probably untrue, but not unthinkable.

Magician Jeff McBride stood up from his seat and walked to the back of the room. He knew what was coming and wanted no part of it—meaning, he didn't want to be selected as Calvert's volunteer. I sank down in my seat and pulled the brim of my cap over my eyes. I didn't want to be picked, either. I couldn't stop thinking about how I felt during Keith Barry's Spike performance and what Barry had told me about being in control.

Calvert walked through the crowd, closer and closer to me. And sure enough, he stopped right in front of me and he motioned for me to join him onstage.

"I'm terrified of the devil!" I said, loud enough so the guy could hear it over the ominous music—I mentioned he was ninety-seven, yes?

Either my comment didn't register or Calvert didn't care. The guy didn't budge; he just stood there pointing his finger at me.

"I really don't feel comfortable going onstage for this one," I told him. "Sorry."

He made a come hither gesture.

"Really," I said, "*I don't want to do it.*"

He put his head next to mine and whispered in my ear, "It's fine. I'm not really going to slice you."

"I'm sorry, but no," I told him in no uncertain terms.

"Kid, my music cue is running out."

"*No,*" I repeated.

He gave me a disappointed look, and so did the rest of the magicians. Then Calvert walked over to the Asian guy who'd assisted him with the previous trick. Calvert positioned the guy on the table and cut his head off with the buzz saw. Not really, of course—it was a trick—but given Calvert's method, let's just say that I feel spectacular about my decision to abstain from participation.

After the performance, Calvert lectured on his methods, on his philosophy of magic, and on life in showbiz.

"If you're interested in one of my books or DVDs," he said, "and you want to pay me now, that's great. But if you don't have the money tonight, I accept IOUs. In all my years of doing this, I've never had a magician not make good on an IOU."

When the lecture ended, a younger magician, AJ, invited me to do an interview before his webcam. He and his friends Jeremy and Craig do a live broadcast on StreetOfCards.TV from Gary Darwin's magic club each week.

"Tell the viewers at home why you wouldn't help the great John Calvert with the trick," AJ said.

"When I was a kid," I told him, "I used to perform an arm chopper trick. A simple chopper trick that only an idiot could mess up. And I messed it up. I didn't cut my hand off, obviously, but I hurt myself bad. And I vowed that I'd never go onstage for any type of cutting or sawing trick."

I told that story—that white lie, let's call it—because I didn't want to admit the truth. I didn't want to admit that I was afraid Calvert would mess the trick up. I didn't want to admit that I didn't trust the guy. I didn't want any more looks of disapproval. (The StreetOf-Cards viewers have webcams, too.) I told the story hoping to garner sympathy from the online community.

But it didn't. I knew that because I could read the chat room comments:

What a sissy.

The guy's 97. Show some respect, new guy.

What do you have to say for yourself, sissy?

"Well," AJ said, "what *do* you have to say for yourself?"

"Want to hear one of Darwin's cough jokes?"

"It's going to be packed." I said.

"That's the point," Kiana replied.

I hadn't seen Kiana the escort since we'd met at LAX, but one Thursday night I wanted to go out and couldn't find anyone to go out with. So I gave her a call.

"So . . . no working the crowd tonight?" I confirmed.

"I don't want to work; I just want to go have some fun, if that's all right with you."

"It's all right with me. But can we even get in? It's TAO's Industry Night."

"I always get in," Kiana said.

"Yes, but can you get *me* in, too?"

"We'll find out."

In other cities, "Industry Night" (the night that bartenders and servers visit other bars and clubs) usually falls on Sunday. On the Las Vegas Strip, temporal constructs such as "Sunday" or "weekend" are virtually meaningless; in Las Vegas it's always the weekend for the tourists, never the weekend for the locals. It's always Industry Night for some club workers, because the clubs and lounges in the major hotels have different schedules. JET at Mirage, for example, is open on Thursday through Saturday, closed Sunday, but open on Monday. Pure at Caesars is open Friday through Sunday and also Tuesday. Blush at Wynn Las Vegas is open every night except for Sunday. And CatHouse at Luxor is open on weekends and on Wednesday.

Unlike Industry Night in other cities, Industry Night in Las Vegas wasn't set up for the benefit of the people in the industry; it was set up as a tourist trap. Vegas tourists always want to hit up the popular, busy clubs. During the week, there aren't enough tourists to pack every venue, so the major clubs eased into a tacit agreement whereby they consolidate their extra bodies (club workers who've got the night off) in particular clubs on particular nights. That way, no matter the night, tourists always have at least one packed venue to patronize. That's why the clubs allow workers from other clubs in for free—not out of the goodness of their hearts, but because the only way to draw midweek tourists is to have some bodies already inside.

On Monday the place to be is JET at Mirage and XS at Encore, on Tuesday it's Pure at Caesars, on Wednesday it's LAX at Luxor, and on Thursdays it's "Worship" at TAO.

The line at TAO made the line at JET look like the line of Disney World's Enchanted Tiki Room. The Venetian's Grand Canal Shoppes' upper floor was packed with hundreds of twenty- and thirtysomethings re-adjusting dresses, fixing heels, slapping hands, waving club passes, waving money, and doing everything else they could to attract the bouncers' attention. The main line wove all the way around the escalator bank. A separate mob of about one hundred stood by the door, hoping to bypass the line. There were at least a dozen bouncers keeping both groups in check.

Like Oxana said, for a lot of people, this is what Vegas nightlife is all about.

And somehow we're going to get in?

"We're going to walk to the front," Kiana said, "and you tell them you work at TAO in New York."

"They'll ask for a pay stub."

"We'll tell them that we're visiting LA and we weren't planning on stopping by Vegas, so you didn't bring one."

Kiana and I pushed through the mass of people, as if we had the right. When we got to the ropes, we had a stroke of luck: The bouncer was ushering in a group of about ten, half guys and half girls. We tagged onto the end of that group past the ropes.

It all happened so fast.

Success! We're through!

Then I caught a dirty look from one of the guys in the group. "Those two aren't with us!" he called to the bouncer, who had by then moved on to another group.

Kiana grabbed the tattler's forearm and pleaded, but

he was determined. The rest of the guy's group had entered the club and they were calling for him, but apparently he was less interested in having fun with his friends than he was in ruining our night. He tapped the bouncer on the shoulder and kept tapping him until the guy finally turned around.

"What is it?"

"Those two"—he pointed at us—"the Asian girl and the white guy. They're not with us."

We smiled.

"He works at TAO New York," Kiana said. "And I'm Hawaiian."

Presumably Kiana was correcting the guy who called her Asian, not banking on TAO having some sort of Hawaiian girl quota.

"If you worked at TAO you wouldn't be sneaking in behind these guys," the bouncer said. "Now get to the back of the line with everybody else."

We looked to the line, then we looked to the hotel entrance, and there wasn't much question as to which way we should walk.

"I didn't want to go to TAO anyways," Kiana said on our way out. "They're assholes there."

We crossed Las Vegas Boulevard and got a table at Caesars Palace Shadow Bar, a place at which women dance behind illuminated screens. We ordered drinks and I told Kiana about my kiss with Zella, about our subsequent dates, about her promise ring, about Austin her boss, and about her early departure from Bellagio to Mandalay to meet with Austin and a "prospective client."

Kiana's verdict: "She's fucking him."

Without any deliberation whatsoever.

"So you think that modeling thing is a lie?" I asked.

"Maybe, maybe not; she might be modeling for him, too—I'm not saying she's lying about that. But she's definitely fucking him."

The thought had crossed my mind. I mean, I'm not an idiot. It would explain why Austin didn't like her visiting friend, Craig. It would explain why he tapped her on the shoulder to stop her from talking with me. It would explain the late-night text messages.

"Vegas will be good for you," Kiana said. "It teaches you how the world works. But until you figure things out for yourself, here's a general rule: If you think somebody you're interested in is sleeping with somebody else, they are. And I'm sorry, but that promise ring is just bullshit. I thought you were supposed to be an expert on lying."

"I never claimed to be an expert on lying."

"It just surprises me that you believe everything she's telling you—or that you're even considering it."

People make awful lie detectors. We all think we can tell when somebody is lying to us, but scientists have proven otherwise over and over again. Researchers Michael Lewis and Carolyn Saarni left a group of five-year-olds in a room with their favorite toys and told the children not to look at the toys. The experimenters left the room and came back after a few minutes. Hidden cameras revealed that 85 percent of the children looked at the toys, but only 38 percent of them admitted to doing so.* Lewis and Saarni showed the kids' parents videos of their children saying whether or not they'd looked at the toys. The researchers asked the parents to judge whether their kids were lying or telling the truth. The parents were right just half the time.

In another study, University of California psychologist Paul Ekman showed videos of people either lying or telling the truth to professionals known for their truth-detecting abilities (polygraph operators, robbery investigators, judges, and psychiatrists). Ekman asked the professionals to identify who was lying and who was telling the truth. Like the parents, the pros couldn't beat the coin flip test.

I told Kiana about these experiments in an attempt to prove I wasn't as naïve as she thought. She wasn't paying much attention, though; she seemed more interested in a middle-aged guy across the bar, sitting by himself and playing with his BlackBerry.

"That guy over there wants me," she said.

"How do you know?"

---

* The children who looked at the toys and then lied about having done so had higher IQs than the children who looked at the toys and admitted to it. Also, the girls lied more often than the boys did. Also, compared to the girls who admitted having looked at the toys, the girls who looked and claimed they didn't smiled more and showed more signs of relaxation. Discuss.

"He's staring at me, and when I look at him he doesn't look away. He knows I'm working, too."

"How does he know you're working? He sees you sitting across the bar talking with me. He probably thinks we're together."

"Go on about the lying stuff more. I'm listening."

"No, you're not."

"Just keep talking."

Texas Christian University Professor of Psychology Charles Bond asked people from sixty different countries, "How can you tell when somebody is lying?" The results were as consistent as they were incorrect: eye aversion, nervous hand gestures, shifty seat position. Yeah, *none of those things indicate deception*. Psychologist Richard Wiseman wrote: "Liars are just as likely to look you in the eyes as truth-tellers, they don't move their hands around nervously, and they don't shift about in their seats (if anything, they are a little more static than truth-tellers)." According to Wiseman, this is the real way you can determine whether somebody is lying:

> When it comes to lying, the more information you give away, the greater the chances that some of it will come back to haunt you. As a result, liars tend to say less, and to provide fewer details than truth-tellers. . . . Liars often try to distance themselves psychologically from their falsehoods, and so they tend to include fewer references to

themselves, and their feelings, in their stories. . . .
When it comes to relatively unimportant information, [liars] seem to develop superpowered
memories and often recall the smallest of details.
In contrast, truth-tellers know that they have forgotten certain details and are happy to admit it.

"Rick," Kiana said, interrupting my deception lecture, "I hope you're as good at this lying stuff as you
claim, because—"

"I *never claimed*—"

"You might have to do some right now."

"What are you talking about?"

"With this guy."

"What, you want me to pretend to be your pimp?"

"Actually . . ."

"Absolutely not. It's illegal, for starters."*

"No, really? I thought they just took me to jail those
times because they were bored."

"I'm not even sure I see a distinction between pretending to be somebody's pimp and actually being
somebody's—"

"He already thinks you're my pimp."

I looked down to see what I was wearing.

---

* Prostitution is legal in the state of Nevada but illegal in the city of Las Vegas.
It's illegal in any Nevadan county with over four hundred thousand residents.

The guy across the room pointed his index finger back and forth, between Kiana and me. He seemed to be asking whether we were together. Kiana slowly shook her head from side to side. Maybe she was right; maybe he did know she was working.

He walked over to us.

Now, I'm familiar with a lot of explicit pickup lines (e.g., "You know what would look great on you? Me," "You might as well sleep with me because I'm going to tell everybody we did anyway," "The word of the day is 'legs.' Now let's go back to my place and spread the word."), but I've never even imagined one as explicit as this gentleman's: "You look like a thousand-a-night girl."

He meant that she looked like a prostitute who charged one thousand dollars per night.

Kiana didn't respond.

She, I deduced, was negotiating.

"Don't tell me you're a two-thou-a-night girl," he continued. "No way you're two thou a night."

Kiana turned away from him and back to me. All part of the negotiations process, I assumed. I stood up to walk away; I had no desire to be part of whatever was about to transpire. As I stood, the guy said to Kiana, "If he really loved you"—he indicated me with his eyes—"he wouldn't let you do this."

Guess he didn't think I was her pimp after all.

"Tell you what," Kiana said to the guy. "How about we go back to your table, you buy me a drink, and we talk things over."

"Why don't we talk business in my room. I've got a suite."

"One step at a time."

"I don't like discussing business at the bar," the man said. "I wouldn't want the bartender to get the wrong idea."

"That's why I've been tipping him with twenties," Kiana said. "So he doesn't get the wrong idea."

The man looked shocked.

"If twenty bucks is a big tip for you," Kiana said, "you can't afford me. Too bad; you're actually kind of cute. . . ."

"Spare me the flattery; I'm a businessman."

"Then let's talk business."

I was offended, and not only because Kiana was doing business right before me after she'd told me she wouldn't. I was also offended that she'd never engaged me in repartee like that.

The man escorted Kiana back to his table, and I walked to the poker room. Kiana found me after a half hour and said, "Can you keep yourself entertained tonight?"

"Kiana, I don't want to hang out with you when you're working. I don't feel comfortable being a part of this."

"Yeah, I can tell. But you know, you don't have to say it like that."

"Like what?"

"You're supposed to be the nonjudgmental one."

"Again, I wasn't making any judgments; I just told you before that I don't want to be a part of . . . *this*."

"Anyway, I came here to tell you that Simon picked up our tab."

"Simon's a classy guy."

"Verdict's still out. I'll let you know tomorrow. I'm going to hang out with him tonight, so I'll just take a cab home. Don't worry about me."

I woke up the next day and found this text message from Kiana: *2300.*

She meant that Simon had given her $2,300.00.

Guess Simon was wrong about that two thou a night.

8. Something You Can Do
with a Hundred Dollars

The most popular topic of conversation at the poker table is poker. How annoying is that?

The second most popular topic of conversation is sports—"Did you catch the score of the game?" being the operative question. Now, I enjoy playing sports as much as the next guy, but I rarely have the patience to sit through a televised sporting event. I definitely don't have patience to keep track of who's injured, who's having a good year, and who just got traded. The fact that I don't keep track of this stuff *blows men's minds. Men can't comprehend* that when it comes to monitoring professional sporting teams, I don't have the attention span of a Buddhist monk on Ritalin.

The first few weeks, whenever somebody started a conversation about sports with me at the poker table I went along with it:

"You catch the score of the game?" they'd ask.

"No, I was at dinner. Totally forgot about the game. Let's ask somebody else," I might say.

This usually led to a topical sports conversation. So a couple weeks later, I changed my approach:

"Did you catch the score of the game?" some guy would ask.

"Which game?" I'd reply.

"The [ostensibly obvious team]," the guy would say.

"Oh, I don't follow the [ostensibly obvious team]; I'm more of a [sports team I cared about in fifth grade] guy."

The trouble with that approach was that it usually led to a discussion about the current state of the sports team I cared about in the fifth grade.

For a few weeks, I started telling people, "I don't follow sports." But that only brought on conversations about what was wrong with me/my alleged superiority complex (i.e., "You think you're better than us because you don't watch sports?").

And finally, after a couple more weeks of trial and error, I discovered the number-one best thing you can say to avoid a sports conversation:

"Did you catch the score of the game?"

"I'm gay."

Like a charm. Every time. It's best to say it as if you're offended (subtext: *How dare you force your heterosexual questions on me? I'm a human being, damn it*).

The third most frequent topic of conversation at the poker table is women. As more and more women enter the game, these conversations happen less and less (because they're so often sexist in nature), but when a table is filled with ten guys the topic comes up. I don't think the average poker player is more sexist than the average man. I think that if you bring any ten men into head-to-head competition, they're going to feel a pressure to assert their masculinity and their assertions will often manifest themselves in the form of misogyny. That's meant to explain, not excuse.

Maybe it's because I'm the last one at the table to participate in these sexist conversations (or maybe it's because I'm clueless), but *something* about my character motivates other men to offer me unsolicited romantic advice. Happens all the time.

Happened one Sunday afternoon in late winter at the Bellagio poker room. I was sitting at a low-limit game drinking white wine and waiting for Zella to meet me for dinner.

"You've been quiet on the topic," the investment banker with tinted glasses sitting next to me said. The topic was girls and girlfriends.

"Just focusing on the game," I replied.

"You got a girlfriend?" he asked.

"Not sure."

"Not sure? What does that mean?"

"I guess it means that it's complicated."

"Well, it shouldn't be. Make it simple. That's the trouble with most guys—they complicate things. But it's usually simple. You've got to show your girl that you're a man."

"And how do I do that?" I asked, with as much disinterest as I could muster.

"Stop drinking white wine for starters," he said.

The table shared a great laugh at my expense, and I gave everybody a dirty look—at least I tried to. Dirty looks lose their effectiveness when you have to rotate your gaze 180 degrees.

A couple dozen hands later, I flopped a straight flush.

For those of you who don't play poker, flopping a straight flush is kind of like getting a hole in one: it's very unlikely, but if you play long enough, it'll happen. I held the nine and king of spades, and the dealer turned over the ten of spades, jack of spades, and queen of spades—in order and everything.

Because I was sitting at a 4-8 table, I could only bet and raise in increments of $4 in the first betting round. That doesn't sound like much, but the pots can add up fast. In the past hour, one or two pots had grown to over $150, and one of them grew to about $200. And considering there were still five other players in the hand with me, I stood to make a lot of money with my monster hand.

I bet $4.

And everybody else folded.

Net profit: $17 ($20 minus tip and rake★).

I turned my cards faceup, hoping to at least gain some sympathy from the other players (sympathy stem-

---

★ The "rake" is the portion that goes to the casino.

ming from their understanding that a fantastic poker hand like a straight flush deserves more than $17), but I didn't gain anything. One guy chuckled, but nobody else seemed to care.

I'm never playing poker at Bellagio again.

Yeah, that's what I told myself after every losing session. But week after week, I returned to play. It was just a five-minute drive for me. But some poker players fly across the globe to play Texas Hold'em at the Bellagio. The other casinos do everything they can to compete. The Palms poker room holds daily raffles, which poker players can enter if they get a diamond flush. The Monte Carlo poker room offers players complimentary Jolly Ranchers.* But these poker rooms do so to no avail; players flock to Bellagio.

An economist might guess that the good poker players would emigrate from Bellagio to the other poker rooms until the concentration of good poker players at all the other rooms equaled the concentration of good players at Bellagio. And if poker players were perfectly rational beings—they come pretty close—they probably would. But any economist worth his weight in calculators† would tell you that even the most rational among us are not always fully rational in the economic sense.

Think of the Bellagio poker room as a pyramid

---

* Though, suspiciously, there are never any watermelons in the bowl.
† This is a common saying among economists, I assume.

scheme, minus the scheme. The money pours in at the bottom, at the low-limit 4-8 games, and the successful 4-8 players take their cash over to the 8-16 tables and lose it to the more experienced players, who, in turn, lose it to the 10-20 no-limit pros . . . and eventually every chip ends up sitting in front of Phil Ivey, eight-time world series of power bracelet winner.

The Bellagio poker room has forty tables split up into three sections. There's the main area, where poker peons like me and James Woods* play. Past the main floor you'll find the raised-platform high-roller games. This is where poker pros go to empty the wallets of traveling businessmen, overpaid entertainers, and foreign dignitaries. One dealer told me she often sees businessmen losing twenty thousand dollars per session.

Across from the raised platform you'll find Bobby's Room. This is where top poker professionals go to play against other poker professionals. Even most foolhardy millionaires know they don't stand a chance against these guys. Bobby's Room isn't open every night, but when it is it usually houses the biggest poker game in the world.

Bobby's Room is named after Bobby Baldwin, the then-youngest World Series of Poker Main Event bracelet winner. In 1998, Steve Wynn made Baldwin president of the Bellagio, and he went on to become the

---

* Saw him there one night, looked like he was winning a lot. Other celebrities I've seen playing in Vegas: Larry Flynt, Hank Azaria, Richard Kind.

CEO of MGM MIRAGE and then CEO of City-Center. I've never seen Bobby Baldwin in Bobby's Room, but I have seen grandfather of poker Doyle Brunson in there a couple of times. He usually sits in front of a giant portrait of himself.

How's that for intimidation?

Like Lance Burton, Doyle Brunson and Phil Ivey are honest deceivers. They might bluff you, but they'd be the first to admit this.* In a magic show, audience members enter into a tacit agreement with the magician whereby they agree to be deceived. In a poker game, players enter into a tacit agreement with each other whereby they agree to bluff one another and be bluffed. So it shouldn't surprise you that I've learned a lot about deception by playing poker. The most important lesson I've learned about deception from playing poker is this: *People are bad at it.*

Scientists have proven this much. Researchers Robert Feldman, Larry Jenkins, and Oladeji Popoola gave subjects two glasses of liquid, one of which tasted good, the other of which tasted bitter. They told the subjects to convince a panel of observers that both drinks tasted equally good. Some of the researchers' subjects were first graders, others were seventh graders, and others were college kids. The first graders performed the worst; they

---

* Some poker players actually go out of the way to "advertise" their bluffs, hoping other players will then call down their legitimate bets (bets made with legitimately good hands) more frequently.

couldn't help but grimace when tasting the bitter liquid. The group that performed second worst wasn't the seventh graders, though; it was the college students. The college students acted as if they liked the bad-tasting drinks even more than the good-tasting drinks, and once the observers figured this out, the college kids were not much better than the first graders at disguising which drink was which.

Novice poker players are like the college students: When they have a good hand, they act like they have a bad hand; when they have a bad hand, they act like they have a good one. This observation forms the core of "poker tell" expert Mike Caro's philosophy: *Weak means strong, strong means weak:*

> Most people are prevented from living the life they want. In childhood, they're required to do chores they hate. They grow up having to conform at school. As adults they must shake hands they don't want to shake, socialize with people they dislike, pretend they're feeling "fine" when they're feeling miserable, and *act* in control of situations where, in truth, they feel frightened and unsure. . . . On an unconscious level, they think, Hey, I'm so phony that if I don't act to disguise my poker hand, everyone will see right through me! And that's why the majority of these pitiful

people are going to *give you* their money by always acting weak when they are strong and strong when they're weak.

Caro says that when a player has a strong hand she'll act like she's going to throw her cards away, set her chips in the pot weakly, and shrug as if to say, *What the heck?* Sometimes she'll look away from the table, as if there's something else more interesting going on in her mind. When a player has a weak hand, she'll stare at the cards on the table intently, reach for her chips when other players are betting, and throw her chips into the pot with unnecessary velocity, sometimes staring you down as she does.

But not always.

If a poker player suspects you're on the lookout for what Caro calls "tells from actors," she'll act strong when she has a strong hand and weak when she has a weak hand. And if she suspects that you realize that she's trying to avoid "tells from actors," she'll act weak when strong and strong when weak. Instead of sending "false tells" like these, most professional poker players simply keep their mouths shut and try to keep a poker face.

I'd been looking out for tells from actors and false tells all night, but it wasn't doing me much good. My chip stack had dwindled from $140 to $40, and so I bought in for another $100, and then my stack dwindled back to $40. I blame the loss on Zella. If she'd have shown up when she said she was going to, I would have left the room earlier.

After rebuilding my stack to $120, I finally saw Zella walk past the poker room. She was wearing a long khaki coat over a short khaki dress, and that kind of made it worth the wait. The investment banker saw her, too, and apparently she made quite an impression with him:

"See, to get a girl like *that,* you need three things."

I braced myself for what was to come, figuring it would be ironic on at least two levels. The first thing was money. He actually said that—technically, I think he said "bankroll," which is a poker term—but I missed the other two things because I was busy sending Zella a text message: *Find me in the poker room and give me a big kiss.* She found me and gave me the kiss I asked for. She must have understood there was a reason behind my asking, because she made a big show of it. I'd hoped the kiss would leave the investment banker speechless or apologetic, but he didn't seem to care.

I got a rack and gathered my chips.

"How'd you do?" Zella asked me on our way to the cashier cage.

"I did okay."

Gambler-speak for *I lost about a hundred bucks.*

"Tell you what," she said. "This Friday, dinner's on me. We'll do something fancy."

At the cage, Zella put her hand on my shoulder and handed me a *What to Do When the Fun Stops* brochure.

But I didn't have a gambling problem; I had a losing problem. I didn't need to learn how to quit gambling; I needed to learn how to do it better.

The first thing you need to know about Mike "The Mad Genius of Poker" Caro is that he's not mad—not literally and not figuratively. He's very nice and very sane.* He might look crazy—his unkempt hair resembles that of a mad scientist—and he might act crazy, but that's only because he wants people to think he's crazy, not because he is crazy. In fact, Caro might be the most calculating poker player in the game—again, both figuratively and literally†; he developed the first commercial computer program that allowed users to analyze poker situations. He's also managed two poker rooms and written a dozen books on poker.

So I guess the second thing you should know about Mike Caro is that the man can play cards.

"Let me buy you lunch," I offered. I figured whatever poker knowledge he had to offer me would be worth at least the price of our meal.

"Let's let the casino buy lunch for both of us," Caro

---

* Related: One night I saw Riviera's topless review show, *Crazy Girls,* with Oxana. After the show, we hung out with the dancers. All sane, many dull.
† If you think I'm overusing the phrase "both figuratively and literally," check out the biography *Andre the Giant: A Legendary Life* (i.e., "He was larger than life, both figuratively . . .").

Appearances can be deceiving.

suggested. "I played a little blackjack last night, and they told me I could get it comped."

"Shall we do the buffet?"

"Let's."

The Rio Hotel's Carnival World buffet offers more than 370 items. I filled my plate with barbeque ribs, unpeeled shrimp, crab legs, sweet potato, green beans, cantaloupe, honeydew, banana custard. Then I thanked Caro again for lunch, adding, "I'd heard you were really nice."

"I'm probably the most liked poker player in history, and let me tell you why: I cheer for my opponents. I mean, I *genuinely* cheer for them. I want them to win pots. See, if you cheer for your opponents, either you'll be on the winning side or you'll get a consolation prize and win the pot yourself."

"You might genuinely cheer for them, but you don't genuinely want them to win," I pointed out.

"I *do*."

"That sounds like self-deception to me."

"Everybody thinks poker is all about deception. That's a common misconception, that it's all bluffing and lying. But there are times to be deceptive and times to be straightforward. And if you confuse those times, you're in trouble. Deception works against you any time it's not required. Straightforward is always the ideal—in life and in poker. If I have to be deceptive, it means I'm varying from my best strategy. It's a sacrifice to be deceptive."

"Maybe you could give me an example of something that's deceptive but a sacrifice. . . ."

"How about this: I burn hundred-dollar bills at the table."

"Those things get in my way, too."

"What I'm doing," Caro explained, "is trying to convey to people that I don't care about money. Remember, in the games I play, a hundred dollars is a small amount. It's really not that much money. But when you see a hundred-dollar bill burned, you remember it—more than, say, if you saw somebody tip a cocktail waitress a hundred bucks."

"And when people think you don't care about money . . ."

"When people think I don't care about money," Caro continued, "they call me with marginal hands every time I bet. They figure I've got nothing and that I'm betting for the heck of it . . . because money means nothing to me. But I usually play strong cards, so I end up making a lot more than a hundred dollars on them. And I never burn more than one bill at the table. That's the good thing about burning hundreds: I don't have to do it more than once. Once I do it one time, all the players who see it will hype my supposedly 'crazy' reputation. And every time somebody new sits down at the table, somebody else will say, 'He burned a hundred-dollar bill! He does it all the time! This guy is crazy!'"

Maybe that's why nobody called me when I bet my straight flush at Bellagio: I wasn't projecting a silly/crazy "table image." I'd been inadvertently projecting the opposite table image: cold and calculating. Hell, between hands I was reading an 880-page book called *Metamagical Themas: Questing for the Essence of Mind and Pattern* by a philosopher named Douglas R. Hofstadter. You can't get more calculated appearing than that.

I began to tell Caro about what had happened at Bellagio, but I cut myself short when I remembered that Caro is famous for not listening to what poker players call bad-beat stories—stories of unfortunate luck.

"It's true; I don't listen to bad-beat stories," Caro confirmed, "but you're welcome to tell me yours. And I'll nod sympathetically and pretend to listen, and that way it works for both of us; I'll get to use my time more productively and you'll get the illusion of sympathy."

"Let's do it," I said.

"Huh?"

"I want to tell you the story still."

"Go ahead, I guess."

"So, I was playing four-eight at Bellagio," I began, "and I flopped a straight flush. I had the nine and the king, and the board filled up with a ten, jack, and queen. . . ."

Caro nodded sympathetically and massaged his forehead.

". . . I was in early position, and there were five people in the pot with me. And the pots at this table were huge. One hundred, two hundred—big, big pots. One after the other. So I was pretty sure I was going to make a lot of money with this hand."

Caro grabbed his head, then opened his arms and held his hands palms up.

". . . I bet the flop, and guess what happened. Everybody folded! Not one caller!"

I nodded, indicating that my story was through.

After a beat, Caro declared, "Poker is terrible!"

"I know!"

"Just terrible. So you're done?"

"I'm done," I said, "So when did you stop listening to bad-beat stories?"

"A while back. One of the reasons I don't listen to bad-beat stories is that I have the ultimate bad-beat story myself. I wrote about it in *Card Player* magazine, actually, and sometimes, when somebody starts to tell me a bad-beat story, I say, 'Tell you what: you go read my story in *Card Player,* and if your bad-beat story is better than that, I'll listen to it.'"

"You must have had a pretty bad beat."

"Well, let me tell you how bad it was. . . ."

I hate hearing bad-beat stories, too. Telling them is fine, but listening is just awful.★ To me they're on par with traffic stories (e.g., "I was in the right lane heading north on Decatur, and the truck was going west on Sahara, about to make a left, I think, and when I honked, the guy in the center lane, who had his *right* blinker on . . ."). So as Caro started to tell me his bad-beat story, I started to zone out. But I didn't want to be disrespectful to the guy, so I continued to pound away at my MacBook keys.

Here's my unedited version of Caro's bad-beat story:

asdkl asfjasdf adsj; af asd k; fasdj fa ;kf;fa k;sdfas;
ads f;a sd kfj; asd fka s;fk asd f;as ;kfas; fa sdfj

★ I'm not a hypocrite. I'm just a better storyteller than most people.

ads;kf jas;k l fj;ads kfj; asd fasd f ask fjad s;kf a;sd k
fa;js fk;las jkl; fja sd ;lkf ajs ;fklasr uasd k;lra
lsd;kj rua u;as ;ta s;d k tua s; dkt a tu ka;stu; as dut
aks;d tkau su kt; asdut ;aksd t;k at dsa t as d; ;tu
k;as t ka; st las dt a sdtu; adkstula stu sad;ktu asd t
kas dt u ad;s tkakd ls tk lu asdtl a skt ;astl alsd kt
kalst d sat; ;aslk t; lk das t;ads tadst a t;l au lf daf
vaut ast ua;dstk ug adgu akls;d gl;ad gu dask gld-
uasg asdu g;daskg asdg a dsg adsu g as gd asdg as
dg ; uaklsd g;a dsg asd g klasdga skd lg.

As Caro went on, I nodded my head and made sym-
pathetic grunts.

He stopped his story short—I think; again, I wasn't
really paying attention—frowned, and said, "You're not
listening, are you?"

"Of course I'm listening," I replied. "Poker is terrible!"

A couple days later, Zella took me to the Wynn and
made good on her dinner offer. She and I descended the
spiral escalators, walked past the Alice in Wonderland–
inspired Parasol Down Lounge, and sat at the table for
two she'd reserved for us at Daniel Boulud Brasserie, a
restaurant situated before Wynn's Lake of Dreams.

The Lake of Dreams is similar to Mirage's Volcano
and Bellagio's dancing fountains in that it's free water-
based entertainment but different in that: (1) Unlike the

Mirage Volcano and the Bellagio fountains, you can't see the Lake from the Strip; you have to walk inside Wynn Las Vegas and through the casino to view it,[*] and (2) you can't describe the Lake of Dreams without sounding like you're on LSD.

But here goes: There's this auto-animatronic frog that hops on top of a giant waterfall and lip-syncs to War's 1975 R & B chart topper "Low Rider." As the serene lake below transforms into a colorful, swirling mess, the frog blinks, moves its head from side to side, and drums its finger to the beat. Then there's a half-hour break. Next a ceramic head pops out of the water and lip-syncs to the 1985 hit "Oh Yeah" by the Swiss group Yello.[†] The head starts out as a Picassoesque woman with a second mouth in place of her right eyeball, but then it turns into a gorilla. Then a half-hour break, then a luminescent red ball falls in love with a luminescent blue ball and purple miniballs pop out and bounce around.

Told ya.

Zella and I ordered a giant cheese platter, and when the server brought it over, he meticulously pronounced and described each selection. With equal meticulousness I forgot everything he said right after he said it. The cheese tray also had a mini-loaf of fig bread, a

---

[*] Story goes, the Mirage Volcano and the Bellagio fountains were built to bring people into the hotels; Wynn's Lake of Dreams was built to reward those who'd already made it inside.
[†] It's the song from *Ferris Bueller's Day Off* ("Bow bow. Chicka chicka.").

bunch of grapes, a cup of dried strawberries and apricots, a tiny jar of marmalade, and a tiny jar of creamy honey on it. All gone in about three minutes.

"Let's split the burger," Zella suggested. "Or do they have lobster here? We could do that."

"Lobster? Are we celebrating something?"

"We're celebrating your poker loss."

"That's a good way of putting it. Let's get champagne then."

"I don't really drink," Zella said.

"Yes, you do."

"I mean, I had that glass of wine at Bellagio because you'd ordered it for me already and I felt bad, but I really don't drink."

"You must have had ten shots that first night I saw you at JET."

"If I drank all the shots guys bought me while I'm behind the bar, I'd be brain-dead. Those were slipknots—fake shots. I've got them pre-poured and sitting below the bar. They're water, different fruit juices—that's it."

"I thought I saw you give the guy—one of the guys in the suits—one of your shotglasses and he smelled it. . . ."

"Yeah, he asked to. See, some guys know that bartenders don't always take real shots—guys in the industry, guys who know people in the industry—so I soak the rims of the glasses in booze. I have a couple trays of alcohol below the bar. And when a guy says 'You're really going to do it, right?'—something that lets me know he knows about the slipknots—I pull out one of the soaked glasses."

The waitress came by and I ordered us the DB Burger and Diet Cokes in champagne glasses. The waitress wasn't amused.

As Zella handed the menus back to the waitress, I noticed that her promise ring was gone. I'd been holding her hand on the walk over but hadn't processed the ring's absence until that moment.

"Did you break your promise?"

She knew what I was referring to: "Nah, just took the ring off."

"Oh. . . ."

"What, you don't believe me?"

"I . . ."

"If I were going to sleep with someone and lie about it to you—which I have no reason to do, by the way—I'd keep the ring on."

That is, unless you took the ring off so you could make the argument, "If I were going to lie to you about sleeping with someone, I'd keep the ring on," knowing that I'd view it as a good point.

My God, I've been playing too much poker.

Zella was right. It's not like we were in any sort of committed relationship. We were still just getting to know each other. She had no reason to lie to me.

Then again, maybe things were getting more serious

than I realized; a couple minutes before our burger arrived she said this to me: "I think you'd make a good father."

Right outta left field.

"Where'd that come from?" I asked.

"Just thinking out loud. I do that sometimes. You ever think about that?"

"Yeah, I've been in long relationships. Got me thinking about that stuff . . . but usually I keep that kind of thing to myself."

"Well, now you're making me feel insecure. . . ."

"No. I didn't mean it like that. It was a sweet thing to say."

Psychologists Carolyn Saarni and Michael Lewis say that men are more likely to downplay one-night stands and short-term relationships and to exaggerate long-term relationships.*† According to Saarni and Lewis, women are less likely to call men out on their lies (than men are to call women out on their lies) because they don't want to "stir things up." Psychologist B. M. DePaullo argues that women aren't passive; they're actually worse than men at determining when somebody is deceiving them *because* their desire to please has overtaken their desire

---

* Okay, so my "long relationship" wasn't even a year. It was fifty-one weeks and change. I know that because we celebrated our one-year anniversary by breaking up with each other—exchanged gifts and everything.

† Women were more likely to downplay previous long-term relationships and to play up one-night stands. So both men and women tell potential mates what they believe they want to hear.

for truth. Either way, given men's predisposition to tell lies (discussed four chapters back), you might think that women are at some sort of deception disadvantage when it comes to courting. But this isn't the case. . . .

If women are attracted to men who can provide for potential offspring, men are attracted to women who, like Zella, look like they can produce offspring. In fact, to say that a woman is "beautiful" in the conventional sense is to say that she looks fertile. Men are drawn to showgirls, promotional models, bottle girls, strippers, and, yes, Vegas bartenders because they look like they can bear fifteen children but aren't too deep into that process. Without getting too bogged down in evolutional psychology, guys are attracted to fertile women because the guys' male ancestors were. The genetic lines of the guys who were into infertile women petered out long ago.

Just as men present themselves as richer and more powerful than they really are, women present themselves as younger, healthier, and more fertile than they really are—one quick look around the Daniel Boulud restaurant confirmed this much. The female diners weren't showing off fabricated fertility clinic reports—though I can envision this becoming a Miami trend—but they were lying about their age. Not verbally, visually.

First example to come to mind is hair. Like Zella, a lot of women at the restaurant that night had died their hair blond. Blond hair occurs naturally in youth and grows out with age. A woman's hair may turn from blond to red, blond to brunette, or blond to gray with age, but never the other way around. So before hair dye came along, blond hair served as a reputable indicator of youth. Crudely put, if a caveman slept with a blond chick, there was a good chance he'd knock her up.

The caveman's chances were even better if the cavewoman's blond hair was long and lustrous, too. An unhealthy woman's body sends nutrients away from the hair and to the more crucial body parts. As a result, the woman's hair grows thin and dull. Today women simulate long, luscious hair with wigs and with hair extensions made from synthetic substitutes like Kanekalon and Toyokalon. Stylists form the Kanekalon and Toyokalon into wefts, which are clipped, sewn, or hot-glued onto a woman's hair. They stay there until they are unclipped, cut off, or unglued.

Using hair extensions and hair dye (and silicone and Botox and Spanx), the women dining at Daniel Boulud evened out the romantic-deception playing field by faking all the once-reputable indicators of fertility. Men are attracted to women with (obviously) dyed-blond hair because our genes haven't had time to catch up to our intellect. Hair dye hasn't been around that long.

And here's the kicker: Even though I understand that much—I understand that my intellect hasn't had time to catch up to my instincts—it doesn't make me any less attracted to women with blond hair. And not because the media bombards me with highly sexualized images of blondes (as many politically correct talking heads argue); the media bombards me with images of these women because, like I said, I'm predisposed to find them sexually attractive.

Evolutionary psychologists Alan Miller and Satoshi Kanazawa compare this to fast-food advertising. They say that Americans don't consume so many McDonald's hamburgers because we're brainwashed by McDonald's commercials. The commercials just capitalize on our innate preferences. We consume so many McDonald's hamburgers *because they taste good.*

But not as good as those of Daniel Boulud. . . .

After dinner, Zella told me she wanted to go to the bathroom to "fix [her] makeup."★

"I'll walk out with you," I said. "I've got to use the bathroom, too."

We ascended the escalators and used the bathrooms by the front entrance. As I was washing my hands, a group of five guys walked in and the one with the faux-hawk asked me, "Are you buying tonight?"

"Can't afford to buy," I told him.

I'd assumed he was selling drugs.

"Bullshit; your shirt's worth more than my whole getup," he replied.†

★ I'm pretty sure this is girl code for poop.
† The shirt I was wearing cost me around twenty dollars, I think. I bought it a decade ago, in a store at the mall that catered primarily to wannabe skaters. I was

"I can't mess with drugs. If you knew how bad I got addicted to over-the-counter nasal spray, you'd understand."

"I'm not talking about drugs," the guy replied. "I'll fuck you in the ass for two fifty."

Presumably the guy meant $250, not two bucks and change. But given how off my first assumption had been, he could have meant two hundred and fifty thousand. Regardless, it sounded like a rip-off.

"I'll pass. Thanks, though."

"Let me tell you a story," the guy said. "I know this guy who came to Vegas and gave this hooker five hundred bucks. You know what she did for that? She told him to get naked and lie on his stomach. So he did, and then she took out a bottle of lotion, rubbed it into his back, and walked out of the room."

Presumably this story was meant to illustrate the relative bargain I'd receive by doing business with the guy.

"Maybe next time," I said.

On the walk to the valet, Zella said, "I'm too sleepy to drive back to Henderson."

"I can drive you home."

"Yeah, but my car is here. How will you get home then?"

---

wearing it when I first met my ex-girlfriend Victoria, and I remember that because on our second date she told me, "When I first saw you, in that shirt, I thought for sure you were gay." That'll become important in a second.

"I could—"

"I'll just spend the night at your place," she suggested.

So that's how we dealt with that one.

9. Heroic Police Officer Prevents Disguised Idiot from Carrying Out Massive Terrorist Attack

Kiana asked me to join her at Seamless Adult Ultra Lounge. Oxana was out of town, and I wanted to get a woman's opinion on Zella's recent unresponsiveness. Ever since she spent the night at my place (and the two nights after that), she'd been acting distant. Three fun nights together, then nothing, then a ton of talking, then nothing again. I figured Kiana might be able to tell me why.

Seamless functions as a normal strip club until 4:00 A.M., at which point the strippers leave, clothed go-go dancers come in, and the place turns into a dance club. Seamless is free for locals, but the bouncer at the front door didn't believe I was one.

"I'm local. I've been living here for five months," I told the bouncer, wondering how much longer my "four-to-five-week" Vegas vacation could possibly last. "And I'll tell you what," I added. "If you don't believe me, you can call my mom and ask her. She'll tell you all about it."

"Everybody says they're a local," the bouncer replied.

"The ten guys in front of me didn't."

"Everybody except for them."

I texted Kiana and told her to meet me at the door. She told the bouncer, "He's cool."

"Debatable," the bouncer replied.

"Oh, not cool like *that*," she agreed—hardy har har—"but could you let him?"

"He's local?"

"Yes."

The bouncer frowned and let me in, leaving me to wonder whether he was frowning because he had to let me in or because I lived in the same city as him.

I don't like strip clubs. Before moving to Las Vegas, I'd only been to one strip club, one time, and I would have been fine keeping things that way. I don't have any moral reservations; I just think they're desensitizing and depressing.* Guys at the poker table tell me that they can "separate" strippers and call girls from the "real women" in their lives. I don't know what, exactly, they mean by "separate"—I suspect they don't know what they mean by it, either—but I'm still confident they're wrong. I bet

---

* The desensitization of attraction has been proven in the lab by researchers James L. Howard, Myron B. Reifler, and Clifford B. Liptzin, who showed men and women porn movies for ninety minutes a day, five days a week, six weeks total. During the seventh week, the subjects reported a decrease in sexual desire.

most evolutional psychologists would agree with me. The human brain can't help but compare, and when men do compare, their wives, girlfriends, and dates almost always come up short. Not because strippers are always more attractive than men's significant others (though for most guys, the strippers certainly are), but because it's a stripper's job to act exactly how men want her to act (provocative, interested, charmed, aroused).

"I hate it here, too," Kiana told me, "but Simon really wanted to come. I kinda like him."

"*Simon's* here? The guy from Caesars?"

"He's at the bar doing business with those guys."

"What does Simon even do?"

"I don't know for sure. He tried to explain it to me, something with finance, but I can't really follow that stuff. And he might have been lying."

"So you *are* working . . . after you promised me you wouldn't."

"I'm not working! Just hanging out. I'm allowed to do that, aren't I?"

"You mean Simon's not paying you?"

"You don't have to say it like that, but yeah, that's what I meant."

"Oh . . . *good*?"

"Oh, they *hate* it when girls work here."

"That's why you tip the bartenders in twenties, I thought."

"Doesn't work at strip clubs."

Prostitutes compete with strippers indirectly and directly. Many of the high-end call girls are more attractive than many of the dancers and make them look bad by comparison, which presumably cuts down on lap dances. The prostitutes also cut into the business of the dancers looking to go home with their clients. None of the dancers I've met in Vegas ever admitted to going home with customers,* but all of them told me a majority of their coworkers do, so you do the math.

One stripper I'd met at a coffee shop, oh, let's call her Java, told me she pulls fifteen hundred dollars a night—minimum. She works at Spearmint Rhino and usually doesn't even take her top off. Men pay a couple hundred per hour to have her sit at their table and flirt. One part stripper, two parts geisha.

"I hate sports and politics and business," she told me, "but that's what guys want to talk about, so I read the whole paper every day and educate myself."

It doesn't surprise me that girls like Java get bigger tips than a lot of the girls who do take their tops off. Guys give strippers money because they want something from them. If a guy has already received what he's after (nudity), there's no incentive for him to pay more. Plus, the less obtainable a girl is, the more desirable she is. It all goes back to the free pants on the street.

---

* Strippers pride themselves on not sleeping with guys for money; call girls pride themselves on not getting naked before large groups of men.

Only no amount of money will win Java's heart. She's asexual.

"Something like one percent of the population is asexual," she told me. "No big deal to me—I've always been like this—but most guys refuse to accept it. There's more asexual strippers than most guys would care to know."

To me, Java's asexuality makes her job performance all the more impressive. It's like an autistic guy winning a Best Actor Oscar.

No matter how many copies of this book you buy, I'll never make as much as Java or the girls who work at Seamless. I'll almost certainly never make as much as Kiana or her coworkers. And I'll admit it: I'm kind of jealous. *Freakonomics* authors Steven D. Levitt and Stephen J. Dubner offer this explanation for the seemingly unjust salaries:

> The typical prostitute earns more than the typical architect. It may not seem as though she should. The architect would appear to be more skilled (as the word is usually defined) and better educated (again, as usually defined). But little girls don't grow up dreaming of becoming prostitutes, so the supply of potential prostitutes is relatively small. Their skills, while not necessarily "specialized," are practiced in a very specialized context. The job is unpleasant and forbidding in at least two

significant ways: the likelihood of violence and
the lost opportunity of having a stable family life.
As for demand? Let's just say that an architect is
more likely to hire a prostitute than vice versa.

Kiana and I sat down on a sofa near the bathroom
and watched as dancer after dancer escorted patron after
patron to the club's ATM and then to the back rooms.
After a half hour I realized that none of the dancers
were stopping by me to ask whether I wanted to dance.

"Why aren't the girls stopping by us?" I asked Kiana.

"You haven't been making eye contact with them."

"Is that all there is to it?"

"Try it out," she suggested.

I made eye contact with the next dancer who walked
by us and she plopped right down on my lap.

"Hi," she said.

That was fast.

"Hi," I said.

Now, if I weren't sitting so close to this girl (i.e., under
her), I would have thought she were wearing novelty
buckteeth. But they were her teeth, all right. Otherwise
she was attractive—and that just made the teeth stick
out even more.

"What do you do?" she asked, putting her hand on
my inner thigh.

"I'm a magician."

I didn't say "lawyer" because I didn't want her to

think I had money. I said "magician" hoping it would scare her away like the plague. Didn't work.

Now, here's what the stripper *wanted* to say in response: *Maybe tonight I could show you a magic trick,* but here's what her limited English allowed her to say: "I can do a magic, but my magic is a different magic. I can do a magic for you . . . but it is . . . different than the magic that you do with friends. I do a magic . . . with a part of you that is . . . different."

She was gyrating back and forth as she was saying all that, by the way.

"Ohhhhh!" I responded, after what I was pretty sure was the end of her awkward monologue, as if I'd just at that moment figured out what she was getting at.

"No thanks," I said, indicating Kiana.

"I can do special magic dance for two people," the dancer offered.

Before I could say no, Kiana saw a dancer she knew and called out: "Alex!"

"Hey!" the girl replied.

"Alex was one of the first girls I met when I moved here," Kiana told me. "At TAO, actually. We almost lived together."

The bucktoothed stripper walked away, and as she did Alex told us, "It's her third or fourth night. I give her a week, tops. I just hope she makes enough for oral surgery before she goes; did you notice?"

"We noticed," Kiana and I said in near unison.

"Yeah, but even if she got that fixed, I don't think she'd be good at this. Takes a certain type, you know?"

"Alex was trying to convince me to work here when I first moved here," Kiana said.

"I still think you'd be great at it," Alex said. "You've got the right personality. And if you've got the right personality, this is the best job in the world. Most guys don't realize that. They're like, 'Oh, you're a dancer. Poor thing. Let me help you. Let me save you.' But I've done all kinds of jobs before—service stuff: temp jobs, officey-type things—and I swear I have more power and control doing this than anything else I've ever done. That's actually my favorite thing about this job—the control. Well, the money first, but then the control. When I'm dancing, I control everything. When we start and stop, the money, the guys. It's like, *Don't feel sorry for me, buddy. I'm making twice as much as you are. So let* me *help* you."

Kiana had once told me the functional equivalent about her gig: "I make the decisions, I pick the price, I have veto power over what I do and who I do it with"— something like that. And it raises an interesting question: *Who's controlling whom?* I'm not convinced Alex and Kiana have it right—nor is feminist Ariel Levy, author of *Female Chauvinist Pigs*. Levy describes female chauvinist pigs as "women who make sex objects out of other women and of [them]selves." She says that by viewing women as nothing more than sex objects, the female chauvinist pigs have not actually acquired any power or control:

> I tried to get with the program, but I could never make the argument add up in my head. How is resurrecting every stereotype of female sexuality that feminism endeavored to banish *good* for women? Why is laboring to look like Pamela Anderson empowering? And how is imitating a stripper or a porn star—a woman whose *job* is to imitate arousal in the first place—going to render us sexually liberated?

I agree that laboring to look attractive is probably a roundabout road to liberation (and possibly a dead end), but on the other hand, I don't see anything inherently wrong with laboring to look like Pam Anderson . . . unlike Levy:

> Instead of hairy legs, we have waxed vaginas; the free-flying natural woman boobs of yore have been hoisted with push-up bras or "enhanced" into taut plastic orbs that stand perpetually at attention. . . . The women who are really being emulated and obsessed over in our culture right now—strippers, porn stars, pinups—aren't even

people. They are merely sexual personae, erotic dollies from the land of make-believe.★

I shared the CliffsNotes version of Levy's argument with Alex—I'd just finished reading it, so it was fresh in my mind—but she wasn't having anything of it. Alex left to go grind on the lap of some guy wearing a Red Wings jersey.

"Could you ever date a stripper?" Kiana asked me.

"I have."

"Was it tough?"

"Yeah, but not because she was a dancer. The one dancer-related thing was, this one time she gave me a lap dance and I freaked out because I started thinking about how many other guys she'd given dances to. Other than that, wasn't an issue."

"And how's the current girlfriend?"

"Yeah, I was hoping we could talk about that. I don't know if Zella's my 'girlfriend,' though, but things are . . . well, I don't know how things are. She spent a couple nights at my place, and they were amazing, but then she went two days without returning my calls, and then we talked *a lot*, and then she went MIA for . . . it's been about a week now."

★ Saying that strippers "aren't even people" is as nasty as it is untrue. But even that wasn't Levy's silliest attack. At one point in her book she criticizes *Girls Gone Wild* for being "utterly plotless," which to me is kind of like criticizing a Sudoku puzzle for its lack of character development.

"When you talked, did she say what she'd been doing those days after you spent all that time together?"

"She said she had this last-minute modeling gig, and I was asking her about it, but she said she didn't want to talk about it because it put her in a bad mood."

"Yeah, she's definitely fucking him. I told you that, Rick. I've got a lot of friends who model, and they know about their gigs long in advance. But even if it's true, that something came up last-minute, why didn't she just call you?"

"I know."

"Have you thought about spying on her?"

"No. . . ."

"No, you're right, bad idea. Okay, hmm, what if you invited her to something specific, far in advance, and see if she comes?"

I took Kiana's advice and sent Zella this text: *Having a huge party on Sunday. You in?*

I assumed Oxana would be okay with this.

Zella responded right away: *Hell yes. I'll let bossman know in advance. just needed some notice is all. :)*

Me: *You sure?*

Her: *I PROMISE!!!*

Kiana walked over to Simon and then back over to me.

"Simon says we have to go," she reported.

" 'We' as in . . . ?"

"*You* can stay if you want, if you want to contribute to the oral surgery fund over there, but I've got to go."

"Where you off to?"

"Don't know. Simon didn't say."

"You didn't ask?"

"Nope. He just said we're leaving."

And who's controlling whom?

"She said she could come to the party, by the way," I told Kiana.

"Good. Now let's see if she does."

"And what am I supposed to do before then?"

"Don't call her. If she's got another guy right now, you want her to pick you, but you can't make her. I can see you smothering her—you've got that personality. So, yeah, don't call or e-mail her."

"Easier said than done."

"Find something to keep you busy."

"Such as . . . ?"

"Think of something."

In the 1890s, Elizabeth Banks dressed up as a peasant to investigate the working conditions of street sweepers in England. In the 1950s, author John Howard Griffin darkened his skin pigmentation to experience the Jim Crow South as a black man. A few years ago, freelance writer Norah Vincent disguised herself as a man to study sexism and the so-called male privilege. Her book that followed, *Self-Made Man,* became an instant *New York Times* bestseller.

When I began writing, I imagined myself one day

following in these brave writers' footsteps. I imagined getting into disguise, taking to the streets, exposing some double standard or grave injustice with irrefutable first-hand knowledge, and then humbly accepting my Pulitzer, my Peabody, my Nobel.

But that never happened.

Unlike Banks, Griffin, and Vincent, I was never motivated by social equality; what interested me about this sort of undercover journalism was the disguise element—the deception. What interested me was the question, how does it feel to pass as another person? I'd been thinking about that a lot, particularly since my conversation with Steve "Tiny" Daly, the magician who performs in drag.

Sociologists use the term "passing" to refer to the practice of successfully presenting yourself as somebody of a different sex, race, ethnicity, class, or disability status. Some people strive to "pass" in hopes of achieving psychological wholeness (e.g., transsexuals); others do it for social acceptance (e.g., the upwardly mobile, the disabled). Still others seek to pass for very specific reasons. During the Civil War, women bound their breasts to pass as men and fight in battle. During World War II, German Jews tried to restore foreskin to pass as Gentiles and evade concentration camp imprisonment. Mixed-race civil-rights leader Walter Francis White passed as a Caucasian man to gather information on upcoming lynchings. African American FBI agents Kevin and Marcus Copeland passed as Caucasian cruise line heiresses Tiffany and Brittany Wilson to divert a kidnapping plot.

Okay, that last one was the plot of *White Chicks,* but the phenomenon of passing is very real and very common. According to UNLV professor of sociology Michael Borer, "When a person is intentionally trying to act as if she is someone else, we can call this 'parallel play.' This happens more often than we think, especially in cities like Las Vegas where there are so many opportunities to play with one's identity."

Professor Borer offered me some common examples of parallel play: "When people 'dress up' to go out to a fancy dinner (that they've been saving up for), rent a limo for the prom, or buy a knockoff Louis Vuitton bag, or when people 'dress down' to go to a ball game, a rodeo, or a dive bar, they're playing with visual social class distinctions."

I told Professor Borer about the conversation I had with Daly. I told him how Daly said that passing as another person felt "exhilarating," and I told him about my desire to emulate journalists Banks, Griffin, and Vincent. Borer said, "If you do it, be careful. You might realize that your fantasies are 'better' than your realities and end up feeling trapped in yourself. On the other hand," he continued, "you might realize how good you have it by seeing how some identities have been socially stigmatized within the status hierarchy of the dominant culture, like African Americans, homosexuals, the disabled, the aged, the obese. Some 'masks' can be fun to wear, try on, and play with; others can be oppressive, alienating, or downright dangerous."

I drove to a local costume shop to search for ideas. There wasn't much there, just some plastic noses, bushy eyebrows, handlebar moustaches, extra-thick nerd glasses, frizzy wigs—nothing that would fool anybody. I needed something more realistic, so I went to the Internet and expanded my search. It didn't take long before I came across spfxmasks.com. SPFX Masks manufactures over-the-head silicone masks that move with your face. They make scary masks—zombies, vampires, demonic clowns, wolfmen—but they also carry a line of realistic disguises known as RealU Masks. If you've got a few hundred dollars ($589–$809) and a head, you can transform yourself into an old man ("The Elder"), a square-jawed bully ("The Sarge"), an African American ("The Player"), or a tattooed, cauliflower-eared gangster ("The Thug").

"If you just want to pass as somebody else and stay under the radar," SPFX founder/mask sculptor Rusty Slusser advised me to "go for The Elder. He attracts the least amount of attention."

I told Slusser why I wanted a mask, and he replied, "That's nothing; you should hear some of the requests I get. A couple months ago I got a call from some guy who got barred from attending his son's football games because he started a fight with the referee. The league got a restraining order against him, and he called me and asked for a mask so he could watch his son play incognito."

"Which one did you give him?"

"I turned him down. These things are for entertainment, not breaking the law."

FedEx delivered the mask and "sleeves" (the fake hands/arms that SPFX customers can purchase separately) a couple days later. I removed the sleeves first and was taken aback by how closely the silicone flesh resembled that of my paternal grandfather: tan with a speckling of dark brown and off-white. My grandfather earned this skin tone by alternating between the Michigan cold and the Florida sun for two decades, and Slusser had somehow duplicated it with paint, practically overnight. The hands were crinkled and the wrist bones protruded slightly.

Next I removed the mask and put it on. I positioned the eyeholes before my eyes and the nostrils below my nostrils. I tucked the neck and shoulder flaps under my shirt and then walked into the bathroom and looked in the mirror. I'd never felt so existentially disoriented in my life. My brain couldn't accept that the old guy in the mirror was actually me. Once the existential shock died down, I examined my new face. My cheeks had drooped with the decades, and two flaps of skin hung loose from my chin. The right side of my nose exhibited a slight red irritation, and faint blue veins popped from my temples. My lips were dark purple and slightly chapped. My bushy gray and white eyebrows splayed in every direction. I'd aged fifty-five years in sixty seconds.

I put on a white cotton overshirt, nylon pants, white socks, blue Crocs, and a Panama hat. Then I opened the front door and set out to retrieve my mail, as an octogenarian.

When I was on the way back from the mailbox, an SUV passed by and the driver nodded. He didn't give me a funny look or point or call the cops; he just acknowledged my presence and drove off. I rushed back to my condo—in retrospect, this was out of character—and poured myself a cup of tea in celebration. I know the driver hadn't gotten a good look at me, but still I felt the tingly guilty pleasure you feel when you get away

Young man / Young man wearing SPFX's silicone Elder mask

with something naughty but harmless in the grand scheme of things. It was the same feeling I get when I bluff a pot at the Bellagio poker tables.

A couple days later I visited the Salvation Army secondhand store and purchased a walker. I also bought a pair of off-white pants and an ugly light brown shirt. That night I got into disguise and headed toward a nearby bus station. Now, I've never been mugged or held up in my life, so I usually don't think twice about walking around the city at night. As a twenty-seven-year-old male, I don't make an ideal target for would-be criminals. But as an old man, I realized, I made a much more enticing potential victim. I left my cell phone and wallet at home for security, but still my nerves got the best of me and I headed home before reaching the station.

I was equally self-conscious when I visited the nearby Desert Breeze park the following day. For a while I just stood there and watched the teens in the skate park. At first they ignored me, but eventually I drew points and whispers. I don't think the kids suspected something was up; they just wondered why the old guy with the walker was staring at them. I got the same reaction from the toddlers on the playground and their understandably concerned parents.

I ambled over to the dog park and let myself through the gates. I sat down on a bench and received another nod. This one was from a seventy-something Doberman owner, standing about ten feet away. I sensed the nod was of the peer-to-peer "Howdy, fellow old-timer" variety, and I nodded back.

A couple minutes later, a chocolate Lab ran up to me and began licking my mask. It must not have tasted good, because the dog walked away before his owner could get out her apology.

"Sorry," she said. "He's a licker."

"What's his name?" I asked.

I didn't use the stereotypical old man voice, but I did lower my register and retard my speaking speed.

"Morpheus."

"You're a *Matrix* fan?"

"Yes . . . ," the woman answered tentatively, probably surprised that I'd picked up the reference.

"My grandkids, too."

Later that afternoon I got back into costume, drove to Las Vegas Boulevard, and walked around in front of Bally's, Bill's Gamblin' Hall, and O'Sheas. Typically when I loiter in this part of the Strip, a part where many people happen to be intoxicated, I get high fives from frat guys and occasional flirtatious eyebrow arches from girls holding frozen drinks. But when I was wearing the old-man mask, everybody ignored me.

When I was a kid, I used to have this reccuring nightmare that I was invisible to everybody around me. Nobody could see me or hear me—not my friends, my parents, or even my dog, Jake. I'd jump and scream and get no reaction. Now, I'm no psychologist, but I think this has something to do with being an only child/needing attention. And in Slusser's old-man mask, I wasn't getting any of it, and honestly, it was starting to piss me off. I felt less like I was wearing an old-man mask and more like I was wearing a cloak of invisibility. I wanted to cry out, *Somebody pay attention to me! I'm a person, too,* but instead I took the mask off.

SPFX should really be marketing these things to paparazzi-swarmed celebrities.

The next day I wore my old-man disguise to Walgreens to see whether I could buy a bag of Werther's Original Hard Candy without being "read." I handed the cashier a twenty and fumbled a bit with the change he gave me in return. When the transaction was done, he gave me what I thought was a suspicious glance—the first one I'd yet elicited. I couldn't stand not knowing whether he realized something was up, so I got into my car, removed the mask and arms, and walked right back into the store, still dressed in my old-man pants and ugly shirt. I bought a second bag of Werther's to see how he would react.

He didn't; false alarm.

"You selling a lot of Werther's today?" I asked, more confident in my disguise.

"Was . . . was that you?"

"Was who me?"

"Never mind."

Later that day I ran into Oxana's friend Inessa by the

mailbox. She was walking her dog and I was in costume. I hadn't seen her for a few months.

"Hi, Inessa," I said, making no effort to disguise my voice.

"Hi," she replied, backing away little by little. It's not every day that some octogenarian you don't recognize knows you by name.

"Don't you recognize me?" I asked, hoping to mess with her a little bit.

"No," she answered, picking up her pace.

"Inessa—wait! It's me. Rick."

She froze.

I removed the mask and sleeves. Inessa was scared when I had the mask on, but my God you should have seen her right after I'd taken it off. I explained my project and I gave her a hug.

She was shaking.

"So I fooled you?"

"I need . . . I need . . ."

"Are you okay?"

"I honestly need a minute here," she said. "That was really freaky. I'm still freaked. . . . I just need a minute, okay?"

Guess she hadn't "seen it all," after all.

I've been performing magic for two and a half decades, but I've never fooled somebody so badly. I doubt most the guys at Darwin's magic club had, either.

During my time as an old man, I went through the

same emotions that Banks, Griffin, and Vincent went through: initial excitement, paranoia, sadness, and ultimately triumph. My adventures also confirmed Professor Borer's prophecy: I realize how good I have it as a member of our youth-dominated, youth-obsessed culture—particularly when it comes to meeting new people and making new friends. Steve Daly was right, too: Deceiving somebody as to your whole identity is a rush.

I was ready for the ultimate test. . . .

Even before I put the mask on I was having second thoughts.

I can't fool these guys. They all know about disguise for one reason or another. If they don't work in drag or moonlight as an impersonator, they teach a course called Special Effects Makeup on a Walmart Budget.

I took a deep breath and pulled the silicone over my face. Then I put on the off-white pants and the ugly light brown shirt. I shook some baby powder into the prosthetic "sleeves" and then slipped those on as well. Next, a tattered suit jacket and worn shoes.

If this doesn't work, I'm going to look like an idiot.

By the time I got into my car, my heart was racing. I was starting to sweat a little, too. At least, I thought I was starting to sweat a little, but it's hard to know whether you're starting to sweat when you've got silicone on your face, hands, and arms. I turned the car's air-conditioning on high and pointed all the vents at my face. The cool, recycled air shooting through the mask's eyeholes, nostril holes, and mouth hole felt good, but there wasn't enough of it.

Of course, if I do pull this off, I'll have their respect forever.

I reached into the glove compartment and pulled out a pair of sunglasses. I'd been debating the sunglasses for a while. On the one hand, they covered up the slight ridge where the mask met my eyes. On the other hand, well, who wears sunglasses into a bar at night? Misguided twentysomethings, that's who. Definitely not octogenarians.

But better to look funny than get caught.

Pulling out of my driveway, I started worrying about things I hadn't considered before, like what would happen if a police officer pulled me over. Would I have time to remove the mask before he approached my car? Almost certainly not. Removing the mask was a dozen-step process involving untucking, unpeeling, undressing. So I drove to the bar extra-slow, extra-cautious—the way I'd drive if I were as old as I was pretending to be. And as I drove, I began to imagine the worst-case scenario. . . .

Excuse me, I imagined the police officer saying. *Could you please step out of the vehicle?*

What's that, young-timer?

I said, step out of the vehicle, Gramps.

Is something wrong?

You're wearing sunglasses and the sun's been down for hours—that's what's wrong.

Since when is wearing sunglasses a crime?

It's not, but it's enough to make me suspicious, and my suspicion warrants . . . Say . . . something looks funny about your face. Is that . . . is that a mask?

How dare you?!

It is a mask.

I imagined the officer unclipping his walkie-talkie and speaking into it: *Attention all units: We've got a five-twenty on Desert Inn and Sirius. I'm going to need backup for this one. Suspect is armed and dangerous.*

I'm not armed.

Step out of the vehicle and put your hands in the air!

These aren't even my hands. Here, let me show you. . . .

I imagined myself reaching up the sleeve of my suit jacket to access the top of the silicone prosthetic. I imagined the officer assuming I was reaching for something else, pulling out his gun, and shooting me in the face. The following day, the headline of the *Las Vegas Review-Journal* would read: "Heroic Police Officer Prevents Disguised Idiot from Carrying Out Massive Terrorist Attack."

The horrific vision came to an end as I arrived at Boomers. I removed my walker from the trunk and entered the bar. I didn't get carded.

I made my way to the back room, and when I walked in, everybody looked at me . . . and they kept looking.

Odd, as I'd grown so used to being ignored while wearing the mask.

They're probably just wondering who I am. They're wondering if I'm a hobbyist or some famous magician from the 1950s they should recognize.

While new magicians showed up at Darwin's magic club every week or so, few of them were in their eighties. The guys in their eighties had generally been around for a while; eighty is a little late in the game to start magic as a hobby.

I approached Steve "Tiny" Daly's table first. I looked through his merchandise and he looked at me . . . skeptically. I think he knew what was going on. I'd told him a couple days back that I'd gotten my hands on an old-man disguise. But I hadn't gotten more specific than that, and I definitely hadn't told him I planned to come to Boomers wearing it. Still, he was looking as though something was on his mind. He looked as if he wanted to ask me a question. But he never did.

"How's it going?" I finally said.

"Pretty good," Daly replied. "And you?"

"Been better."

After fifteen or twenty seconds, I moved on. As I did, I saw from the corner of my eye Daly tap the shoulder of the guy sitting next to him. Then he pointed at me.

He knows.

I caught another point from the other end of the

room. And then another. And then one from Velcro Shoes. And then Velcro Shoes walked over to Daly and, I'm pretty sure, started asking about me.

Something is wrong. Did I put the mask on improperly? Is it bubbling up in the back?

I did a quick double check and found that I had put the mask on properly, that it was not bubbling up in back.

Is it the sunglasses? It must be the sunglasses. They were a bad decision. Too suspicious.

I took the sunglasses off and slipped them in my breast pocket.

Everybody's still staring.

In Mr. Washington's eighth-grade English class, I read Edgar Allan Poe's "Tell-Tale Heart," the story of a neurotic murderer who chops up the body of this old guy and hides it beneath the floorboards. When the police show up, the murderer hears the old man's heart beating through the floorboards. The beating gets faster and faster and louder and louder, and eventually the murderer can't stand it anymore and he confesses to everything.

Of course, the old man's heart wasn't *really* beating through the floorboards; the hallucination was a manifestation of the killer's guilt.

And that, I realized, *is probably what's happening to me. People aren't* actually *staring or pointing at me. I'm just imagining it. Their "looks" and "points" are a manifestation of my worries. In reality the glances are benign and the hand gestures are conventional.*

After all, if they knew it was me in a disguise, they'd say something. They'd crack a subtle joke or use a double-entendre, anything to let me know that they'd figured things out. They'd want to go on the record as having figured things out, so I couldn't later claim I'd fooled them.

The younger magicians called me to the StreetOf-Cards.TV webcam for an interview. I'd told them (and no one else) beforehand that I'd be coming to Boomers in an old-man disguise, and they promised me they wouldn't tell anybody. I fully trusted them to keep a secret. They're magicians, after all.

For our interview I had to face away from the thirty or so magicians in attendance. I had trouble concentrating on my words because I could feel the magicians' eyes burning a hole in the back of my silicone mask. What I do remember is saying nasty things about the StreetOfCards.TV viewers. Guess I was still bitter about their comments following John Calvert's show.

After the interview, I was ready to take the mask off. But I couldn't do it in front of everybody. I was ready to go home. But I couldn't leave yet. See, I'd only finished the first act of my performance.

I went back to my car and removed the jacket, the fake arms, and then the mask. Turns out I was wrong: I thought I'd been sweating a "little bit," but in actuality I'd been sweating buckets. My face was dripping, my eyebrows were slick, and my hair felt the way it does when I step out of the shower. I soaked up the sweat with an extra T-shirt I'd brought, changed my clothes, and went back inside for act two.

That time I got carded.

I walked to Steve Daly's table first.

"Hey, Steve," I said. "Long time no see."

"Where you been?" he asked.

I couldn't tell if his question was genuine or if he was placating me.

"Around," I replied.

I walked over to Velcro Shoes and said, "How you been?"

"I've been okay. You just getting here now?" he asked.

"Yeah," I said suspiciously. "Had a late dinner . . ."

"Well, good to see ya."

I walked around the room and got one, "Look who finally shows up," and one, "Thought you weren't gonna show."

They're fucking with me, I thought. *The reason they didn't say anything earlier was that they were playing along. They knew the whole time.*

"Let's cut the crap," I said to Velcro Shoes. "You knew it was me, right?"

"I know *who* was you?"

"The old guy in the jacket. Who was standing right here at your table like twenty minutes ago."

"Old guy in the white pants."

"Right. It was a disguise, and you knew that. Just admit it."

"What do you mean I 'knew that'? You're trying to tell me that was you?"

Is this guy looking for a Tony or what?

"Don't patronize me. Just admit it so we can move on."

"You're saying that was you? I'm saying bullshit."

"Oh, come on," I said, "You were looking at me funny. And I saw you pointing. And I saw you and Daly talking."

"I was asking him who the new old fart was."

The magicians never revealed whether they knew my secret (magicians are stubborn like that), but as time goes by, I become more and more convinced that I had them fooled. I become more and more convinced that I deceived the deceivers.

Now tell me that doesn't deserve a Pulitzer.

In the book *How to Play in Traffic,* Penn & Teller write: "Magic is for boys who are not popular. Magicians are either asexual or desperate. They pick people from the audience so they can flirt with them in public." I wish I could say I'm above doing that, but my eighth-grade talent show performance in which I "randomly" called on this particular girl to tie me up for a rope escape—one that I specifically created as an excuse to flirt with her in front of the entire graduating class—begs to differ.

Remember, that was thirteen years ago, back when David Copperfield was with supermodel Claudia Schiffer, back when I saw magic as a surefire method of meeting and seducing beautiful women.

After Lance Burton married blond showgirl Melinda Saxe and David Blaine dated *Sports Illustrated* swimsuit model Josie Maran, the magic/seduction plan seemed foolproof. But for me it was flawed. If I showed a girl too many magic tricks, I found, I turned into a circus monkey. Girls like to watch circus monkeys, but they rarely date them. They give them peanuts, not phone numbers. I realize this much now, just as I realize that Copperfield, Burton, and Blaine are the exceptions. And it's not the fact that they're magicians that attract women; it's the fact that they're famous millionaires with their own TV shows.

Since moving in with Oxana, I'd spent a lot of time with her friends—dancers, models, and other girls who were probably popular in high school. We got along surprisingly well, so I was left to figure out whether magic has gotten cooler, whether the girls have grown more accepting, or whether that thing they say about the meek and inheritance is actually true.

I devised a plan to test out those theories. I convinced Oxana to invite her friends to the party to which I'd already invited Zella and a bunch of guys from Darwin's magic club. She agreed, and we billed the event as "The Showgirls & Magicians Ball"—S&M Ball for short. We drove to Walmart and Michaels and acquired all the things you'd expect to see at a fancy ball: three-dollar wine, crepe paper, *Happy Easter* balloons (deeply discounted), and Bagel Bites. Then we tied the balloons to the lamppost and taped crepe paper from the balcony to the staircase.

The magicians arrived around 10:00 P.M. Hoping to facilitate intergroup contact, Oxana encouraged them to make name tags for themselves. She helped create stage names for all the guys, except for those who already had them, like Grendel, Blink, Bizzaro (the guy who teaches the Special Effects Makeup on a Walmart Budget course). Oxana's friends showed up around 11:00 P.M., and as they stepped through the front door one thing became instantly clear: Showgirls take theme parties seriously. One girl wore a silver sequin dress topped off with a red feather boa. Another wore a shimmering gold dress that she'd borrowed from a Tryst go-go dancer. A third wore pearls over lace lingerie, and a fourth wore her prom dress.

By 11:30, Zella still hadn't arrived.

A few mimosas into the night, I formally welcomed our guests: "Good evening, ladies and gentlemen, and welcome to the first-ever Showgirls and Magicians Ball. Now everybody please head to the dance floor."

The girls assembled by the fireplace, but the guys didn't budge. Either they thought I was joking or they were terrified.

"Guys, seriously, get over here and partner up."

I know how to play one slow-dance song on the keyboard: "A Whole New World." I learned it because my natural singing voice sounds indistinguishable from the Disney version of the beloved Arabian pauper Aladdin. This works out well when I'm covering "One Jump Ahead" or, uh, the "One Jump Ahead" reprise, but I've yet to find a karaoke bar with those options. I switched on my seventy-six-key Casio, rotated the knob to "Electric Piano #2," and sang. A UNLV bio major who performs in a casino cover band on weekends covered Princess Jasmine's vocals and hand gestures. As the key changed from D to F and the laughter died down, the magicians and showgirls clasped hands and waists and began to sway. So perhaps the theory about the meek's inheritance was true.

After a little more music and a lot more cocktails (but still no Zella), the Backyard Brawl Magic Competition commenced. Think *8 Mile,* but much dorkier. AJ from StreetOfCards.com twisted his arm around 720 degrees, Craig located four showgirl-selected cards at once, and Bizzaro produced a cube of Jell-O and pushed a red silk through his palm.

The showgirls voted Bizzaro Best Performer, and Oxana presented him with an industrial-size tub of neon green hair gel I'd picked up at the dollar store and then wrapped in expensive wrapping paper. He hoisted it over his head and reveled in the applause.

Even though everybody in attendance had a great

time, I'm reluctant to call the ball a smashing success for two reasons: (1) There were at least a dozen single people there and no numbers were exchanged. (2) Zella never showed up. Instead she sent a text message: *In AZ right now. Had emergency and needed to drive out there. Im SO sorry and WILL make this up to you.*

Yeah right.

10. Something George Clooney Might Do
in a Clark Gable Biopic

It was Saturday night and I was up almost three hundred dollars at the Mirage 3-6 limit tables. Around
3:00 A.M. I started to lose focus. I was thinking less and
less about the game and more and more about Zella
and about whether I should stop by JET and see her on
my way out. She was supposed to be working that night,
but, I realized, it might look creepy if I stopped by un-
announced. Zella still hadn't told me what the Arizona
emergency was, let alone "made it up to me." Instead
she sent me a text message that said: *I can't begin to tell
you how happy I am to have you in my life right now.*

She was talking the talk but not walking the walk.

I'm sure Artisan the PUA and Kiana would have told
me to leave her alone, to wait until she contacted me,
to forget about the whole thing, to move on. But I was
in The Mirage already—it's not like I drove there to
see her—and I had to walk past JET to get my car. Plus,
I had all sorts of free JET entry passes—one of which
I brought—and at 3:00 A.M. there wasn't going to be a
line.

So in I went.

Zella was there all right, and from the way things looked, so was everybody else in Las Vegas. She looked surprised to see me, but only for a split second. By second two, she was mouthing, *I'm sorry,* in my direction. I'm not sure if her apology was meant to cover missing the party or her ostensible inability to talk to me. Of course, Zella had plenty of time to flirt the pants off every other guy in the place—the customers, the male bartender, one of the bouncers. After a few minutes she held up her index finger, giving me what I took to be the "one second" symbol. I took that to means he'd get the chance to talk to me soon. But after a couple minutes I rethought my interpretation.

Lots of guys were standing right next to me, staring at Zella—guys who didn't even want drinks. They just wanted to watch her pour. So after another couple minutes, I was starting to feel like a real chump. I wanted to turn to the guy standing next to me and say, *I'm not just another dude staring at this chick and fantasizing about sleeping with her; we're dating.*

If you're dating, I imagined him responding, *why is she ignoring you?*

Good question, I'd say.

Well, maybe you're not dating, he'd point out.

I imagined pulling out an oxeye daisy and playing the ol' "She loves me/she loves me not" game. I imagined Zella walking over and scolding me for making a mess. Throwing me a wet rag and telling me to clean it up. I imagined driving home and writing a sad poem about it.

Apparently, I couldn't be romantically confrontational even in my imagination.

Poetry, I think we can all agree, is for cowards. Poets have something to say—from what I remember from freshman-year English class, it's usually about sunsets, seashells, or seashells found while walking the beach at sunset—but they're too chicken to come out and say it (e.g.,"I found this shell on the beach"). You might think I'm just saying this because I don't understand or appreciate poetry. You might think that I don't want to admit my own intellectual failings, so I've passed the blame onto a time-tested art form instead. You might see this as textbook self-deception.

Nope, I'm right about poetry being for cowards.

That said, I'll admit there are three poems that don't suck. There's the one that tells you how many days are in each of the months, there's "Casey at the Bat" (which I memorized after I watched Penn recite it on a PBS Penn & Teller special), and then there's this one I learned in choir about the fleeting nature of beauty by William Butler Yeats. It comes from Yeats's collection *The Wind Among the Reeds* and is titled "The Poet Pleads with His Friend for Old Friends." In the poem, Yeats tells his friend that even though she's popular *now,* even though people can't stop talking about her beauty and singing its praises *now,* she shouldn't let it get to her head; she should concern herself with what her true friends think of her—the ones who know her for who she is. Because as she grows older, her beauty will fade to everybody except those who know and like her for who she is.★

Like Yeats's "friend," Zella was young, popular, and much talked about. Her star shone brightest when she was behind the bar.

But I was in front of it. I didn't know what to do, but I knew I had to do *something.* Not just for the sake of my emotional health, but for the sake of our relationship (or whatever you want to call it). Waiting around for her made me look like a desperate chump.

So here's what I did: I swiped a cocktail napkin from the bar and borrowed a pen from one of the bottle service girls. I wrote out Yeats's poem in full:

> *Though you are in your shining days,*
> *Voices among the crowd*
> *And new friends busy with your praise,*
> *Be not unkind or proud,*
> *But think about old friends the most:*

★ I only know this poem so well because we sang it so many times in choir. Really, *I don't like poems.*

234

Time's bitter flood will rise,
Your beauty perish and be lost
For all eyes but these eyes.

Okay, so the poem didn't fit our situation perfectly. I wasn't Zella's "old friend," but I'd definitely known her for longer than the guys crowding around the bar flirting with her did. And I really did want to know her once her shining days were through. Mostly, though, I'd hoped the poem's underlying message (pay attention to *me*, not *them*) might get through to her.

I slipped the napkin under a martini glass, signaled to Zella, and then made my way to the exit. In retrospect, this was a cowardly thing to do, but at the time it felt like the classy, bold kind of move George Clooney would pull in a Clark Gable biopic. Close by the door, I pictured Zella discovering the napkin, reading the poem, inhaling deeply, shedding a single tear, calling my name, and then rushing after me.

Why did I think that? Because I'm an idiot and an optimist. But that's not how it went down.

Right before I left, I turned back and saw Zella pick the napkin up, look at it funny, crumple it up into a ball, and then dispose of it under the bar. Then I saw her do a shot of tequila with Austin and a couple of JET patrons—and I knew it was real tequila because I watched the liquid go from the bottle to the shot glass and then from the shot glass to her mouth. Then I saw Austin whisper something into her ear, and then I saw Zella grab his butt.

That settled that.

It was so obvious.

In the book *Lying,* psychologist Sissela Bok describes the stages people go through when they learn that the wool has been pulled over their eyes:

> Those who learn that they have been lied to in an important matter . . . are resentful, disappointed, and suspicious. They feel wronged; they are wary of new overtures. And they look back on their past beliefs and actions in the new light of the discovered lies. They see that they were manipulated, that the deceit made them unable to make choices for themselves according to the most adequate information available, unable to act as they would have wanted to act had they known all along.

On the walk from the club to my car, I reexamined every moment I'd shared with Zella and reassessed everything she'd ever said to me. Of course, I wasn't 100 percent certain she'd *explicitly* lied to me; when she told me there was nothing going on between her and Austin it might have been true, at the time. Maybe something had developed after that, in which case she was only guilty of deception by omission.

Not that that made anything I was feeling any less painful.

By the time I arrived at my car, I'd passed a dozen gorgeous women—minimum. But the sight of them just depressed me further. I wanted to get away from women and away from Vegas. Suddenly backpacking through Europe didn't seem like such a bad idea.

"How do they even do it?" I asked Oxana the following night. "It's like the casinos are always, *always,* packed with gorgeous women."

"Models."

"They look like they could be," I said.

"No, they *are* is what I'm saying."

"What do you mean?" I asked. "The casinos pay women to walk around and look hot?"

"Sometimes. I've had dozens of those gigs since you've been here—at the Palms, a lot of the time. Usually through this agency called Baker's Babes. Seventy-five per hour. But I've also done a lot of pool party gigs like that, and corporate events."

"And they just pay you to . . ."

"Walk around, drink. At Palms it's mostly in the high-roller lounge, but I've done that in other parts of the casino. I've got the Baker's Babes recruiting brochure upstairs, if you want to see it."

"I want to see it."

She showed it to me.

"A lot of the girls in the shows do this stuff during the day for extra cash," Oxana explained.

"So what happens when you're doing an undercover modeling gig and somebody asks you if you're working?"

"They taught us that if somebody asks us if we're being paid or if we're promo models, we should say, 'I'm just having fun at the casino today. How about you?' Something like that."

"And what happens if the guy isn't happy with that answer?"

"Most of the girls just lie."

"Do you?"

"No. Well, I guess . . . I did once—sort of. I was doing this pool party—not at Palms . . . TAO Beach, I think. So I was basically getting paid to wear a bikini and drink. They used to give us two drinks for free, then it went to three, and now they just want the girls to drink as much as we can, so it's all free. Anyway, these guys were visiting from Jersey—really sweet guys—and I was chatting them up for a bit and I heard one of them say to his friend, 'Back home girls like this would never even talk to us.' And then his friend was like, 'I think these could be models.' And the guy asked me if I was working. I said, 'No.' But then in my head, I thought, *Well, not in the traditional sense.* So is it even a lie if you complete it in your head like that . . . ?"

"Depends on who you ask."

Vegas casinos, I've learned, sometimes recruit under-cover models through outside agencies and sometimes do it directly. Other times they get businesses and mod-eling agencies to hold casting events at their clubs, lounges, and bars—a clever way of bringing beautiful local women through their doors without shelling out any cash.

"I've got a casting event at Blush in an hour," Oxana said. "Did you want to tag along?"

"I'm so bummed right now," I said. "I could stand to be by myself for a while."

"That'll just bum you out more. You've got to get out there and mingle. You need a distraction."

"Maybe you're right. . . ."

Blush was packed, and the girls were younger and blonder and bustier than usual. For a half hour I sat by the entrance and watched guys' faces light up like the Luxor as they walked into the room. But the blondes at Blush weren't there to mingle, or to make new friends, or to drink, or to have fun; they were there to audition for the job of Mixed Martial Arts Ring Girl. A group of local businesses sponsoring a couple of fights had sent some of their workers to serve as judges.

I assumed Oxana's audition would entail walking around in stilettos, holding a card, but as best I could tell, the girls were judged solely on their ability to flirt with the judges without rolling their eyes or gagging. This task was made particularly tricky because none of the judges had name tags identifying them as such, so the girls had to chat up every schmuck in the joint (myself included—poor things), as leading with, "Are you a judge?" would be too transparent (as if the whole "audition" weren't already transparent).

None of the models I spoke with that night knew what, exactly, the ring-girl gig entailed (how many fights there were, how much it paid, et cetera). And from the way the girls told me this, I came to understand that this was par for the course in the Vegas modeling industry: The clients and the agents keep the girls out of the loop. Toward the end of the night, I heard less and less flirting and more and more resignation (e.g., "These shorts are riding up my ass. I'm outta here.").

Oxana forfeited around 2:00 A.M., after all the guys who'd revealed themselves to be judges had informally paired up with girls who weren't her.

"I can't compete with those giant fake tits," she said.

A week later Oxana said that her agent told her that none of the girls were selected. Maybe something fell through or maybe the whole night was a sham.

"I'm so sick of shit like this. It happens *all the time*. I didn't even tell you about the gig I did last week. With some group of guys, something like the Future Capitalists of America or the American Capitalists of

Tomorrow—something generic like that. Basically a bunch of young guys who started different businesses. They were having this party and, according to my agent, they said they wanted girls to pour drinks and do coat check and party stuff like that. But when we got there, after like a half hour, it was pretty clear they just wanted girls to flirt with and make fun of and . . . I don't know if 'sexually harass' is too strong, but that's how it felt. Nobody asked us to pour drinks or do coat check or anything like that. They had other people doing that stuff. They were rubbing against us and pulling us onto their laps. And our *agent* was there, and she wasn't objecting or anything. She just sat there like nothing was happening. I swear to God, sometimes, this business . . . I'm supposed to have this audition tomorrow night, but honestly, I don't think I can bring myself to do it."

"Sounds like it's you who needs the distraction."

"Any ideas?" Oxana asked.

"Actually," I said, "yes. . . ."

Theater critics and stage performers rarely see eye-to-eye. But in the case of *BeLIEve,* Criss Angel's Cirque du Soleil show at Luxor, the critics and the performer agreed on one thing—on that thing Angel had said in the *BeLIEve* promotional video: The show was "unlike anything the world of entertainment has ever seen."

Now, there are three types of bad review a theater critic can give. Joe Brown of the *Las Vegas Sun* demonstrated the first kind—the matter-of-fact "Here's Why This Show Sucks" review:

> Cirque throws everything in its considerable arsenal of stage genius at Angel—the expected array of lush, loud music, expert dancers and aerialists, lavish settings and boundary-breaking special effects, all intended to amaze.
>
> The single most amazing thing about "Believe" is that it's still so boring.
>
> For a reported $100 million, Cirque has bought itself its first bona fide bomb. . . .
>
> A charmless mook, Angel is a rudimentary stage performer—he's barely believable playing himself.

Los Angeles Times writer Reed Johnson demonstrated the second kind of bad review—the snarky "There's Nothing of Substance to Review Here So I'm Going to Review on My Own Cleverness Instead" review:

> Believe that it's unbelievable. Unbelievably bad. In Las Vegas, his [Angel's] mash-up with Cirque du Soleil is a magic trick gone terribly wrong.
>
> If Criss Angel were blindfolded, straitjacketed, run over by a steamroller, locked in a steel box

and dumped from a helicopter into the Pacific Ocean, he still might be easier to salvage from disaster than "Criss Angel: Believe," the gloomy, gothic muddle of a show that officially lurched into being on Halloween night like some patched-together Frankenstein's monster.

Las Vegas Review-Journal writer Doug Elfman demonstrated the third kind of bad review—the "I've Been a Professional Theater Critic for Years and You Expect Me to Waste My Time on This Shit? Look Me in the Eye and Tell Me, *with a Straight Face,* That This Isn't Some Sort of Fucking Practical Joke" review:

> Wooooooooow. Criss Angel's new Cirque du Soleil show is terrrrrrible.
>
> I had heard firsthand from some people who had seen "Believe" that it was abysmal and maybe unfixable, creatively. So my expectations were rock-bottom low (although open-minded), when I saw it Friday on opening night. And yet, it was EVEN WORSE* than how it was described to me. . . .
>
> Obviously, "Believe" was not made to be bad on purpose, and that makes things even worse, since they are TRYING to make a great show.

---

* Caps not mine.

Angel eventually held a press conference and acknowledged that the show had kinks that needed to be worked
out. He mentioned, for instance, that the show's music
had to be adjusted to allow for applause where none was
anticipated.

"People are having a very hard time responding to
me getting cut in half," Angel also said, "because, you
know, they're applauding my death and they don't want
to do that. I'm going to come here tomorrow at noon
and . . . I will work with the director and try to kind of
change the routine a little bit."

Oxana told me that several of her friends had seen
BeLIEve, that they thought it was the worst show they'd
ever seen.

But it was our turn to see for ourselves.

Here's what we saw:

Angel floated down from the ceiling dressed (fittingly) as an angel. From row G, I could see the strings
that brought him down. Now, in all fairness, I'm not
100 percent sure I *wasn't* supposed to see the strings. After all, Cirque du Soleil uses wires to suspend performers in pretty much all of its productions, so maybe
Angel's descent wasn't meant to be a magic trick. Maybe
it was simply a dramatic entrance.

Criss hit the ground, rock music blared, and strobes
flashed. The audience cheered, and the music grew
louder and louder—so much so that I couldn't tell when
the cheering had stopped. A team of Cirque clowns ran

through the crowd and collected gifts that audience members had brought to Angel. Criss had to help one of these clowns, the fat one (the one in a fat suit), back onto the stage, and as he did he grabbed the guy's ass and said, "Now that's a **_HAM_**ful."* The clowns presented Criss with the stuffed animals, the flowers, and the *WE LOVE YOU CRISS* quilt (complete with pictures of Angel's cat, Hammy) they'd collected from the audience.

"How many Loyals are here tonight?!" Criss asked us. "How many people here know who Hammy is?!"†

I'm unsure as to whether I was supposed to realize that the gifts were fake, that they weren't really brought in for Criss. Part of me thinks Angel didn't want me to know this because, well, my God, it's embarrassing. But the other part of me thinks Angel must have realized that critics would discuss the Hammy quilt in their reviews—as they did—and that everybody who read a review that discussed the Hammy quilt would know the gifts were fake.

---

* The capitalization, italicization, underlining, enlarging, and making bold of this word's first syllable is my attempt to textually represent Criss's comic delivery of the line.
† According to a house-of-mindfreaks.deviantart.com (Criss Angel fan Web site) forum post:

> Hamlet nicknamed Hammy is Criss Angel's beloved cat. I doubt there's a person on earth that loves their cat as much as he loves Hammy. Hammy is like a son to him. Hammy is also a magical cat. He can levitate, perform mindfreaks, disappear, and reappear.

So maybe Oxana's cat, Nuzzle muffin, isnt the creepiest cat in Las Vegas.

But maybe I'm not giving Angel enough credit. Maybe Angel foresaw that people who read theater reviews wouldn't be his target audience.

Angel threw a Criss Angel logo wristband into the crowd,* and asked the person who caught it to throw it to somebody else. That person did, and Angel asked the person who caught it the second time to stand up, think of a word, and say it.

"Cute," she said.

Angel pointed to a locked box hanging from the ceiling of the stage and said, "See that box up there. It's been hanging there since before the show opened. Nobody has touched it. I've never performed this trick before, but I wanted to do it tonight because I feel such a deep connection with all of you."

The Cirque clowns unlocked the box and removed from it a tube, which they handed to Criss in ceremonial fashion. The tube contained a large sheet of paper with the word "CUTE" written on it in thick black marker.

It wasn't just the most deceptive (i.e., hardest to figure out) trick I'd ever seen Angel perform; it was also one of the most deceptive tricks I'd ever seen anyone perform. But I'm not sure if anybody else in the audience noticed how damn good it was. I suspect they were busy won-

---

* He mentioned that the wristband featured his personal logo several times. I got the sense that of all his accomplishments, Criss was most proud of this one.

dering whether Angel *actually* expected us to believe he'd never performed the highly choreographed trick before.

Angel asked the woman who picked "cute" for a kiss on the cheek. She puckered her lips and bent forward, and at the last second Criss turned his face and pecked her on the lips.★

After the word prediction, Angel's team rolled onto the stage a human-sized cage with audible electricity shooting through its bars. Angel put on a metal suit, took a few deep breaths, and reached for the cage door. When he touched it, sparks flew everywhere and Angel dropped to the floor convulsing. He'd been electrocuted. The *Be-LIEve* cast rushed onto the stage mid–costume change. One cast member called for a stretcher, another for an ambulance. The audience called out, "Criss!" and, "Criss, are you all right!?" But as the calls went on, it became clear they were actually prerecorded pleas.

Medical officials carted Angel away by stretcher, and a couple seconds later a rabbit puppet hopped up to a miniature microphone and started complaining about the difficulties inherent in working for a magician . . . until a spotlight fell from the ceiling and knocked the rabbit unconscious. The rabbit community at large wasn't happy about the injury. They unionized, and their unionization took the form of an angry ballet number.

★ I remember seeing Angel pull this move on *Mindfreak*. The *Mindfreak* girl liked it more.

The rabbit ballet, I deduced, was Criss's nightmare.

Once the angry rabbits hopped offstage, a new nest of dancers draped in green netting took over the stage. Clusters of red flowers dropped from the sky, landing upright, in bunches. A different warren of rabbits took the stage, but unlike the angry unionized rabbits, these were the friendly, hippity-hop variety. A massive flower bud swooped across the ceiling, and when it hit stage center it blossomed, revealing an aerialist dressed in white. Angel kissed her, but before their love could develop any further, dancing moles took the stage and ruined everything. The moles looked even angrier than the rabbits.

In the middle of the moles' popping and locking routine, Oxana leaned over to me and whispered, "This show has the best dancing I've seen in Vegas."

At the end of the dance number, Criss showed off his Michael Jackson dance moves.

Not bad.

A couple of bits later, Criss got back on the gurney and slowly regained consciousness. He quoted *The Wizard of Oz* (". . . and you, and you, and you were there"), and then, once he realized that the whole thing was a dream, he stood up and shouted, *"Holy shit! Now that's what I call a mindfreak!"*★

★ The line might have been, *"Holy shit! Now* that's *a mindfreak!"* but either way, come on.

Curtain.

Let's discuss:

BeLIEve was doomed from the get-go. Expectations were impossibly high. There's no way Criss could compete with his *Mindfreak* persona. On *Mindfreak* Angel makes Jesus look like a hack. He flies, walks on water, walks through walls, and teleports out of exploding buildings. When *Mindfreak* viewers pay one hundred dollars to see *BeLIEve,* they expect Angel to do the same stuff. The closest thing they get is a video montage of Criss's greatest *Mindfreak* moments (the subtext being *these are all the tricks I* won't *be doing tonight*).

But maybe *BeLIEve* isn't as bad as the critics said. After the show, Oxana and I hung around the theater to gauge audience reaction.

"We don't have anything like this back home," I heard one guy say.

"That was some crazy shit," some other guy said.

Here's where things get interesting: Once the audience had filed out, the ushers closed the doors to the theater. But nobody told Oxana and me to leave the lobby, so we stayed. We heard a voice through the door that led into the theater—the one they'd just closed—so I pressed my ear against it.

"For those of you who haven't heard," I heard a man saying, "we had a breach of security tonight. Somebody got backstage, during the show, and that, ladies and gentlemen, is unacceptable."

I peered through the crack in the door and saw that the guard was addressing the team of Cirque ushers.

"I'm telling you this," he went on, "because it's your job on the line, not mine. If Criss finds out about this, I promise you he's not going to be as nice about it as I'm being right now."

Apparently security was a huge concern at *BeLIEve*. Before we could even go into the theater lobby, we had to walk through a metal detector and check our cell phones at the front desk. It doesn't surprise me that Angel attracts crazy fans. After all, Angel attracts *a lot* of fans. And for this he deserves credit. But that's not the only thing he deserves credit for. . . .

BeLIEve had many great moments (the amazing word prediction, the terrifying electric cage, the gorgeous flower-bed set, the beautifully choreographed badass dance numbers), but in large part, the critics (aside from *MAGIC*'s Rory Johnson) seemed to miss them.

On a similar note, few give Angel the professional credit he deserves. The magicians at Gary Darwin's magic club sure don't. The guy single-handedly turned himself into the undisputed rock-star king of magic through sheer determination alone.

Toward the end of *BeLIEve,* Criss gave a speech about the importance of following your dreams. He said he visited Vegas a decade ago, back when he only had a few hundred dollars to his name. He said that he dreamed about opening a show on the Strip. He said that he worked hard, persevered, and turned his dream into a reality. It came off as schmaltzy and phony, but, ironically, I'm pretty sure every word of it was true.

Criss Angel is living the dream. He doesn't just have the biggest show in magic; he's also got a penthouse suite, a fleet of fast cars, a series of knockout gorgeous girlfriends, *and* wristbands with his own logo. So maybe Angel is right when he says people talk shit about him because they're jealous.

I know I am.

In case things are still unclear, let me spell this out for you: *I'm extremely jealous of Criss Angel and that's why I make fun of him so much.* I'm jealous of his success and I'm jealous of his wealth and I'm jealous of his toys and I'm jealous of his love life. I'm jealous that he dated Miss Nevada and Pam Anderson and Cameron Diaz and Holly Madison. Simply put, Criss Angel achieved the *exact* dream I had as a kid, and I didn't.

So take everything I say about him and his show with a grain of salt. Actually, take the whole shaker. I mock his show's weak illusions, its cliché plotline, and its awful dialogue, but the truth is, if Cirque approached me tomorrow and said, "Criss is sick. We need you to fill in . . . indefinitely," I'd reply, "When do I start?"

One afternoon in Criminal Procedure class, Professor Bandes told the class this joke: The President wanted to

see which of the country's crime enforcement organization was the best, so he released a rabbit into the forest
and sent the CIA, the FBI, and the Chicago Police Department in to try and find it. The CIA paid off a group
of squirrel informants, questioned all the trees, and then
issued a statement saying that rabbits don't exist. The
FBI burned down all the trees and came up with nothing. The CPD sent two detectives into the forest and
after an hour a bear came running out screaming, "I'm
a rabbit! I'm a rabbit!"

The joke is, the CPD is more concerned with ob-
taining confessions than they are with finding the truth.
Now, those of you who haven't taken Crim Pro with
Prof Bandes might be interested to know that it's perfectly legal for police officers to use all types of deception when attempting to obtain a confession. An officer
can tell a suspect, "Your friends copped a plea and rat-
ted you out," even if it's not true. Sometimes, the thinking goes, lying is the only way to get a confession.

Keep that in mind one thousand words from now. . . .

Zella and I met at the Borders a couple days after she
tossed out my napkin note.

"How've you been?" I asked.

"Better."

"What'd you do this morning?"

"Mostly cried."

"Are you going to tell me why?"

"Eventually."

"But not now."

"No."

"When you invited me out to coffee," I said, "I figured you wanted to tell me some things. . . ."

"I do, I'm just . . . This is all very fresh."

"Is it about your job?" I asked.

"No, but I don't want to make this a guessing game."

"Is it about Austin?"

"What *about* Austin?"

She was already getting defensive.

"Zella, you have the right to do whatever you want, but at this point I think I at least have the right to know what's going on between you two."

"Okay, if you have a question, you should ask it."

"What's going on between you and Austin?"

"A long time before I moved to Las Vegas I made the decision to never mix business and pleasure. And I haven't. Does that answer your question?"★

"No, it broadens it to the point of meaninglessness. And you know, you don't seem all that surprised by my question."

★ Psychologist David J. Lieberman, author of *Never Be Lied to Again*, says this:

> When a person is asked a question, if he responds with an answer that depersonalizes and globalizes the question, be aware. Let's say you ask someone, "Were you honest with me about our conversation yesterday?" Watch out if you get a reply like "Of course I was. I would never lie to you. You know how I feel about lying." . . . To sound more empathetic, a liar offers abstract assurances as evidence of his innocence in a specific instance. In his mind the evidence doesn't weigh favorably for him, so he brings in his fictitious belief system to back him up.

"I see what you're getting at," Zella said, "and I see why you're thinking what you're thinking. I'm not oblivious. But I wish you'd be doing less insinuating, because you're way off base here."

"It's just so obvious that something's going on."

"*Something* is going on, yes, but maybe you shouldn't assume so much because maybe you don't know what you're talking about."

"You must have canceled on me ten times in the past two months. With no explanation."

"There are explanations. Those first few times it was because Austin needed me, *for gigs,* and—"

"And he needed you the night I had my party?"

"No, that was something else. The last few times there's been something else going on. That's what I'm trying—"

"Which is?"

"You know," Zella said, "I was planning on telling you, but from the way you're acting, I don't know if I feel comfortable talking about this right now. This isn't what I was looking for this afternoon."

"Well then, I'll talk about this with you: This whole breaking-plans thing, and the keeping secrets—it goes to respect. And when you ignored me at JET, and then threw out the note I wrote you—that goes to respect, too."

"We were swamped! I didn't have time to breathe, let alone socialize with you or read—"

"Oh, but you had time to flirt with everybody else standing around the bar."

"That wasn't flirting! How do you not understand this by now? There's a social component to my job, and when you walked in I was *working, at my job.* I have to make it look like I'm flirting."

"And grabbing Austin's ass is part of your job?"

"I'm not proud of it, but yeah, as a matter of fact. That whole night the staff was joking around about butt grabbing. And that whole night everybody was doing it. Is that my idea of humor? No. But if I don't participate in that stuff and act like everybody else there, then people start to talk, and say that I'm a bitch and that I think I'm better than everyone. So I have to play along. And I *didn't* throw the napkin out, so don't *tell* me what—"

"I *saw* you throw it out."

"I didn't throw it out!"

"You did, and I saw you do it, and I wish you'd just be honest with me about it. But that's a small . . . The big issue here is respect. Like I said—"

"You want to know the *real* issue here?" Zella asked.

"Don't change the topic right now. This is too—?"

"No, this is relevant. This is part of the reason I've been so hesitant to tell you what's . . ."

"Okay," I said. "What's the 'real' issue?"

"The real issue is that you wrote this book about your last girlfriend and you tell me you're writing this book about your life in Vegas, and I have no idea how you really feel about me or if I'm just going to be some character in your next book and you're going to write about all this. That's why I'm reluctant to tell you so much. Like why I'm reluctant to tell you about what's going on right now with me."

Oh.

Zella's accusation caught me off-guard and I didn't say anything in response, which must have looked pretty bad. I stood up and paced around the café, which probably looked even worse. Probably just made me look guiltier. I really did like Zella, independently from everything—who wouldn't?—but I hadn't considered that this might not be as obvious to her as it was to me.

I sat back down.

"So," Zella said, "am I part of your Las Vegas writing project or not?"

I said nothing.

"Straight yes or no," she said.

"Zella, that's a complicated question. I mean, on the one hand, yes, you *do*—"

"Let me cut you off right there. It's not a complicated question."

"It *is* complicated."

"Straight answer."

"I can't give you a simple yes or no."

"Don't you think it's ironic," Zella went on, "that

you're going around calling yourself a master of lying and here you are accusing—"

"I never claimed to be a master of lying! Why does everybody—"

"Whatever, master of *deception*—"

"I never called myself a master of anything. And *I* haven't lied to you. *I'm* not the one who's breaking plans and giving shitty excuses slash no excuses, again and again. And I'm not the one who's sleeping with Austin."

Zella said nothing.

"I know you're sleeping with him. He told me."

It's been one thousand words; that was the lie: Austin hadn't actually told me anything; I'd never spoken with him.

Zella grabbed her purse and walked out of the bookstore. She left behind her cell phone and a folder. The folder contained bills, an insurance statement, some medical documents from some hospital in Arizona, and an uncrumpled napkin poem.

I hung around the bookstore for a couple hours, waiting for Zella to come back and get her stuff. I didn't examine the hospital documents because I figured I'd overstepped my bounds enough for the day when I called her a liar (wrongfully, turned out) with respect to the napkin poem and then lied about talking with Austin. I eventually left the store, figuring Zella would call when she needed her phone.

By 9:00 P.M., Zella still hadn't gotten in touch, so I called her friend Lena, a server I'd once met at JET whose number I found in Zella's contact list, to see whether Zella was scheduled to work that night.

"I think she's on tonight. She was on as of last night, at least. But obviously her schedule's day-to-day at this point."

"What do you mean?"

"With her dad and everything."

"What about her dad?" I asked.

"She hasn't told you?"

"We've had a strange— No, she hasn't told me."

"Her dad's been in and out of the hospital in Arizona for this brain thing."

"What kind of brain thing?"

"I forgot the word, but I guess her dad went into a seizure. Happened two or three times in the past couple weeks, and he's been in and out of the hospital, doing tests and stuff."

"Was it an aneurism?" I asked.

"That sounds right. I think that's it. Aneurism."

11. The Rest of the Truth

I'd left Zella's phone and folder for her at JET. Lena the server had called me two days later to say that Zella had picked them up.

"Zella says thanks, by the way."

"Meaning . . . Zella doesn't want to talk to me?"

"Right."

I called Zella a week later, but she didn't pick up.

But luckily for me, Dr. Sally Caldwell did.

Caldwell, who teaches at Texas State University–San Marcos, wrote the self-help/psychology book *Romantic Deception*. I told Dr. Caldwell about everything that had gone down between Zella and me—about our fun nights together, about Austin, about how I confronted Zella—and then I asked Dr. Caldwell where I had gone wrong.

"First of all, I generally advise against confrontations. Too many questions can be off-putting. It doesn't take long before a woman figures out, *Hey, this guy is showing signs of jealousy. He might have control issues.* So if you think you're being cheated on, I recommend—"

"I wouldn't say 'cheated on'; we weren't exclusive. I just wanted to see if she was sleeping with this other guy, too."

"Either way," Dr. Caldwell said, "it's usually best not to confront. Sometimes you just have to stand back and see what happens. There's nothing she could have said that would have given you proof that she *wasn't* sleeping with this guy. You can't prove a negative, right? Remember, if you ask somebody a question and they give you an answer, it could be a lie or the truth. But if you stand back and let the data emerge—I've always suggested this as a means of determining whether somebody was lying—you'll probably find what you're looking for."

Dr. Caldwell asked me why I'd gotten so paranoid, so I told her about how Kiana had convinced me with her conviction.

"There's a lesson in that, too: You shouldn't allow other people to define your reality. And this Kiana— she was friends with Zella independently?"

"What do you mean?"

"I mean, when Kiana and Zella got together, were you always around, or did they ever get together and talk just them two?"

"Actually, they've never met. . . ."

"They never even met? Then how did this Kiana girl become so convinced?" Dr. Caldwell asked.

Good question. Here's my best guess: *déformation professionnelle.* That's a French term that describes the tendency to look at a situation from the point of view of your chosen profession. Kiana believed Zella was cheating on me because in Kiana's world everybody is a cheater. Similarly, I believed Kiana when she said Zella was lying to me because since moving to Vegas I'd been spending all my time with deceivers. I started to believe that *everybody* deceives *all* the time. Of course they don't. I don't, for starters. And Oxana had never deceived me. Nor had any of the magicians at Gary Darwin's magic club (outside the context of magic).

Just because magicians are deceptive in one part of their lives doesn't mean they're deceptive in other parts. Think back to my chat with Lance Burton, or to John Calvert's anecdote about no magician ever failing to make good on an IOU. Like Calvert, I've found that most magicians are actually very honest in their day-to-day lives.*

★ In his essay "What a Tangled Web: Deception and Self-Deception in Philosophy" [Michael Lewis and Carolyn Saarni, eds., *Lying and Deception in Everyday Life* (New York: The Guilford Press, 1993), 48], Robert C. Solomon writes:

Lying is not corrupting just because it becomes habitual. But it may nevertheless be true that every time one lies, one makes lying a little easier. First of all, "practice makes perfect," and by practicing lying one learns to prepare better lies and better protected lies. Having to follow through the logical vicissitudes and implications of a seemingly simple falsehood is a remarkably invigorating intellectual exercise, and though this might be a dangerous pedagogical technique for those of us who teach still malleable adolescents, any improvement in one's intellectual acuity will at the same time improve one's ability to tell a successful lie. But of course improving one's ability to lie need not and usually does not increase one's propensity to lie, and why should increasing expertise mark moral degeneracy? Improving one's marksmanship does not make one a murderer and studying locksmanship does not render one a burglar.

That said, deceiving people on a daily basis *does* affect magicians' psyches. But in a different way. Magicians deceive others on a regular basis, so we see how vulnerable the human mind is to being tricked. Accordingly, we're among the most skeptical people in the world. Magicians commonly identify themselves as atheists, agnostics, nihilists, and all-around skeptics. But sometimes I wonder whether we take our skepticism too far. . . .

Remember Marty? The magician/law student who thought I couldn't get backstage at the Kanye West show? Well, Marty got an iPhone the day it came out. Shortly after that, he called and told me this story:

"I'm studying at Caribou, and this guy and girl walked up to my table, and say that they noticed my iPhone and wanted to know if I'd be willing to talk about it for like ten minutes. What I liked, didn't like—that sort of thing. They said they'd pay me ten bucks if they could film the conversation, and I said okay. So we did that, and they gave me the money and I gave them my information—name, phone number, address—and that was that. I kept asking them what it was for, but they said they weren't allowed to tell me. I assumed it was some sort of assignment for some sort of psychology class or something like that because they looked young, but I didn't think too much about it. Okay, a few days later I got a call from a woman who claimed she was working on the new iPhone advertising ads. She said this director—this guy I've actually heard of before—watched my tape and said that I'd be right for the new iPhone commercial. Eventually she asks me for my Social Security number, and I say no."

"Probably a good move."

"She said she needed it to book me a flight to New York for the filming. After I said no, she kept trying to convince me that the whole thing was legit and eventually I hung up on her."

"I've booked flights for other people without their Social Security number," I said.

"Exactly. Me, too. Okay, so that conversation happened the day before yesterday. And then today I got this call from *another* woman who told me she was the director's assistant. She kept saying how much the director liked me and that he insisted somebody call me back and try again."

"You said you knew this director?"

"Yeah."

"From where?"

"Just heard his name, I don't remember where."

"Has he done commercials before?"

"Movies, I assume, if I've heard of his name . . ."

"I mean, this is not how commercials are cast," I said.

"*Right*. Sometimes they do that whole man-on-the-street thing, but that's usually for cleaning products, you know? Not the iPhone."

"I agree."

"So I'm thinking identity theft, and I'm starting to get worried. They have my picture, and I gave them my name and number and address and e-mail, and my signature."

"They probably targeted you because of the iPhone. They knew you had some money. . . ."

"Do you think I should call somebody?"

"Like the police?"

"The police, the FBI, Better Business Bureau?"

"I'd start with your credit card company. Tell them what happened, maybe have them put a lock on your account."

"I'm not being paranoid here, right?"

"Occam's razor," I said. "Which is more likely: Some guys wanted to steal from you or a giant company wants you to be their pitchman for the most awaited toy in history because two kids saw you in a coffee shop and liked your face?"

Marty called the FBI and the Better Business Bureau, but they wouldn't help. Why? Because *the commercial was totally legit*. Because Apple really did like Marty's face. Apple flew him out to New York, put him up in a nice hotel, filmed him talking about his iPhone, and then gave him a nice paycheck. The iPhone commercial was broadcast during the World Series and played again and again on network television for weeks.

Because Marty is a magician and a skeptic, he's always trying to avoid Type II errors.★ He doesn't want to "miss" an instance of deception. In other words, if somebody is lying to him, he wants to catch the lie. When Marty called me, he was hoping to avoid a Type II error. But in doing so, he nearly made a Type I error: seeing deception when there was none.

When I moved to Las Vegas, I, too, was concerned with avoiding Type II errors. I was concerned about missing instances of deception. But as the months went by I became so consumed by learning to avoid false negatives, I overlooked the possibility of making a Type I error, a false positive. I overlooked the danger of seeing deception where there was none. And like Marty, I ended up *making* a Type I error. I thought Zella had lied to me when in actuality she hadn't. And I acted on my mistaken belief.

So in the end, I achieved my initial goal—I met deceivers, befriended them, watched them in action, and learned from them—but I had to sacrifice something big to do it: my ability to trust.

Oxana got fake breasts—sort of. They didn't come from the plastic surgeon's office; they came from a Web site that sells anatomically correct external silicone breasts. The

---

★ A Type II error (also known as a "false negative") occurs when you think that something hasn't happened, but it actually has. A Type II error occurs when a doctor fails to locate a cancerous tumor in a mammogram, for instance. A Type I error (also known as a "false positive") occurs when you think that something has happened, but it actually hasn't. A Type I error occurs when a jury acquits a man of a crime he actually committed, for instance.

breasts range in size from 2" protrusion/2lbs all the way up to 10" protrusion/22lbs.* Oxana's 3.5" protrusion/3.5lbs breasts arrived in a plain white box, which we loaded into the backseat of my mom's SUV. Then we drove to Walmart in search of a bra that would accommodate the new breasts and the old ones.

As we were walking into the store, the elderly Walmart greeter noticed the white box in our basket.

"Are you two returning something?" she asked.

"This is ours," I said. "We're just keeping it in the cart here, if that's okay."

We continued walking, but the greeter wasn't through with us: "Hold on. It depends. What's in there?"

"Medical stuff," I improvised, which sent Oxana into a giggling fit, which definitely undercut the legitimacy of my claim.

"What kind of medical stuff?" the greeter asked—less a question, more a challenge.

"It's really embarrassing," I pleaded. "And if you saw, you'd understand. Is there any way we can just shop today?"

The honest approach did the trick: "Go ahead," the greeter said.

We found the women's undergarments section and searched the racks for the largest bras in stock. Oxana

---

★ The Web site calls the 22-pounders Juggs and says that if you order them "you will have to custom order a super large bra to hold these girls."

walked into the dressing room holding a trio of 38DDs in her left hand and the boob box in her right. A ten-year-old girl in the waiting area saw her do this . . . and then, two minutes later, the same girl saw my same roommate emerge from the dressing room looking as if a horny wizard had cast a spell on her chest. I assume this traumatized the girl for life—that she went home and cried, "Mommy, I don't want to get boobs!"

I had a feeling men would react differently.

To test my theory, we got changed and drove to The Mirage. Before we got out of the car, we did a quick double check for nipple symmetry. The breasts looked balanced and real—meaning they looked like genuine implants. We walked from the parking garage to the poker room. Most men had the same reaction: They looked to Oxana's mammoth mammaries, and then

Oxana before / Oxana after, daring me not to stare at her fake breasts

they looked at me. Presumably they wanted to see what chump had somehow conned his way into this buxom goddess's silicone-guarded heart.

Then they looked back to her chest.

But that wasn't surprising. What surprised me was the way women reacted. Their stares were much more blatant, unapologetic. Perhaps that's because they didn't care about getting caught and had nothing to lose. Of course, the guys had nothing to lose, either—it's not like Oxana was going to pull one of them into the palm tree atrium for a quickie. But many men train themselves to look away from women's breasts because, the men realize, women are turned off by guys who do this.★

"When these women look at me," Oxana said, "I feel like they're judging me. Like they think I'm insecure. They think that I think something is wrong with me."

As we walked out of the casino and down the boulevard, we discovered one group of people that paid my roommate no attention at all: the men and women who hand out pornographic escort cards.

"This is so weird," Oxana observed. "It's the first time they're not trying to hand me those cards."

Now, I've always respected escort card distributors for their nondiscriminatory practices (i.e., they give cards to children, the elderly), but apparently they draw

---

★ Women are much more turned on by guys who make blanket generalizations about what women want.

the line at women with breasts larger than those of the women on the cards. Oxana proposed a theory as to why: "Maybe they figure, *It's a lost cause; she's already got a set of her own to keep her busy.*"

As we walked in front of Rockhouse Bar, one of the club hawkers, a short Asian guy with a tall Mohawk, left his post and weaved through the crowd of neon souvenir glass–holding tourists to get to Oxana. He tapped her on the shoulder and asked her if she wanted to come inside and drink for free. I was standing about ten feet behind at this point, so I saw the great lengths the guy had gone to reach her. But she had no idea. If she did, she surely would have smelled the club's desperation and turned down the guy's specific offer, whatever it was. And the hawker knew that—that's why he waited for her to pass by before beginning his frantic approach.

Moot point; she still turned the offer down.

Another block up, we passed a guy who looked remarkably like me. In his late twenties, brown hair, loosened tie, devastatingly handsome. He gave Oxana a once-over, looked over to me, pursed his lips, nodded approvingly, and gave me a double thumbs-up. It's the kind of blatant gesture you only see on the Vegas Strip, and it made me feel good. Now, I realize I didn't *deserve* the thumbs-up. The guy wrongly assumed that I was sleeping with Oxana (and, for that matter, that her breasts were connected to her body). He wasn't congratulating me for befriending her or for living with her—that's for sure. He was congratulating me on my supposed romantic conquest.

Let me say this about undeserved compliments: They're not as good as the real thing, but I'll still take 'em. As Oxana and I continued our aimless trek, I noticed myself getting more and more positive recognition from men. Most of it came from men walking in groups. Nods of approval, high fives, and looks of astonishment—as if I'd pulled off a great card trick.

I was having a much more enjoyable time than Oxana was. She made clear to me that she'd grown tired of the stares and the points, just as I was growing to like them.

"I need to take these out," she said.

"Not yet."

"I'm feeling really uncomfortable. I thought I could do this, but I can't. Everybody is just staring at my tits."

That's an odd thing to hear from somebody who's performed in a topless show on the Las Vegas Strip, I thought.

"Maybe you should just keep them in a little longer. I mean, think about how much work you put into getting them, and going to Walmart, and us driving all the way out here. . . ."

"My back hurts, and I'm getting hungry. Let's just go into Peppermill, get a table, and I can take 'em out there."

"No!" I said . . . a little too loudly.

"Everything okay, Rick?"

"Yeah. I just . . . I know that . . . if you take them out now you'll regret it."

"I can just put them back in if I want," Oxana said.

"I know, but that might take forever. So maybe we should just walk a little more so you can get a better feel for them."

"What the hell are you talking about?"

"I just mean . . ."

"What's really going on here?" Oxana asked.

What was going on was this: I was passing again, and I was having a grand ol' time doing it.

"Nothing's 'going on,'" I said.

"Is this even about me or are you getting some sort of rise out of this?" Oxana asked.

"*Both?*"

"You're such a fucking *guy*!"

"What does that mean?"

"It means I'm not going to be your arm candy to-night! I thought you were above that stuff."

"You're way off base here."

Actually, she was right-on.

"Okay," she said, "which would you prefer? Do you want to go in Peppermill and I'll take these out there, or should I wait until another big group of guys walks by and then rip these things out of my shirt and throw them at you and cause a big scene and start screaming?"

I resigned and said, "Let's do the first one."

We went in Peppermill, and Oxana removed the silicone globes from her oversized bra and plopped them on the table. Way too big to fit in her clutch. Judging by the laughter—by its force and duration—the tabled boobs were the funniest things the girls sitting across from us had ever seen. The guys sitting at the table behind us, though, weren't having such a fun night:

"I'm just saying, why did we fly all the way from New York to Las Vegas to not get laid? We could have not gotten laid in New York."

They were debating whether they should go to a strip club or get a hooker.

"Are you going to give them Kiana's phone number?" Oxana wanted to know.

"I'm not going to be an accomplice to prostitution, no, but I do wish I could help them. I do feel bad for them."

"Why?"

"First of all, I like the guy who said, 'We could have not gotten laid in New York'—clever wording. And second, I remember how I felt when I visited Vegas in my early twenties."

"What, you couldn't get laid, either?"

"I'm not talking about *sex*—I mean, I couldn't, don't get me wrong—I'm talking about . . . It was a general comment, I guess. For tourists, the idea of Vegas is usually better than Vegas itself."

"How so?"

"Everybody thinks they're going to win and, yeah, get laid, but nobody does."

"That's not true," Oxana said. "Some people . . ."

"I know *some* people win and get laid, but most of the time they just *think* something's going to happen and it doesn't. That's why people spend so much time waiting to get into the clubs and pay so much to get in. They think something magic is going to happen inside, but it never does. And then the guys give so much money to the girls who work there because they think maybe something will happen, but they—"

"Come on," Oxana interrupted. "Tourist guys don't *really* think they're going to sleep with the bartenders and the bottle girls."

"They might know that intellectually, but it goes deeper. There's this gut thing. . . . When a guy sees a half-naked woman so close to him . . . I don't know how to say it right, but basically men have this caveman instinct that tells us that when a woman is *that* close and *that* naked she's available. So when the casinos parade around all these women that aren't actually available . . . I just think that's deceptive on a primal level."

"You're so set on what counts as deception and what doesn't," Oxana told me. "I don't think it's that simple. Deception to you might not be deception to me. Like, you think that my 'undercover modeling gigs'—that's what you call them, right?—you think they're deceptive, but I don't see them like that."

"How can you not? It's deception by omission. You're

being paid to pretend like you're not being paid. Seems like an obvious instance of deception to me."

"Well, not to me."

Oxana thought for a minute and then said, "Maybe I've just been in this town so long that I can't see the deception anymore."

I've got to get out of Vegas.

"Although," Oxana said, "is something really deceptive if you know that deception is going on? Like with those guys, talking about going to the strip club—they *know* the strippers don't *really* like them, but they . . . suspend their disbelief, like when you go to a play. . . ."

"Even if you know that deception is going on, you might not realize how, *specifically,* you're being deceived. Like that magic trick I did at the bookstore. Everybody knew it was a trick, but they didn't know how I did it. And not only that; they probably couldn't even guess the *nature* of the method."

"Which was . . . ?"

"The 'volunteers' were guys from the magic club, and they did the sleight-of-hand for me. People know there's deception in the casinos and the clubs and the strip clubs, but they don't know how much. *And* the fact that they know there's deception going on—the fact that they've seen a "behind the scenes" Vegas TV special on the Travel Channel or something like that—only gives them a false sense of security. The people who think they've got Las Vegas figured out are the people most vulnerable to it."

"And what about you?" Oxana asked. "Are you vulnerable?"

"Of course not," I said. "I really do have the city figured out."

After our meal, we hailed a cab and headed back to the Mirage parking garage to pick up my car and drive home. En route, Oxana asked the driver, "Want to feel my boobs?" as if she were auditioning for *Taxicab Confessions*.

"Sure," he said.

She reached forward with one of the silicone breasts in her hand. The driver looked at the breast and rolled his eyes.

Then he rethought things and gave it a squeeze.

In *Never Be Lied to Again* psychologist David J. Lieberman says: "Honesty is at the cornerstone of every relationship, whether it's business or personal."

I'm not so convinced. I dated a pathological liar for a couple of months, and her lies didn't bother me. I knew that I could never believe anything she said, and so I never did, and so I never felt betrayed. Once I figured out this girl's M.O. (saying what felt right in the moment), we got along fine.

When it comes to romantic relationships, knowing your partner's M.O. is key. Only at the very end did Zella reveal to me that she didn't know my M.O.—that she didn't know if I was genuinely interested in her or planning to write about her. Our situation reminded me of Neil LaBute's 2006 play *Some Girls*. The protagonist of the play, an engaged magazine writer, tells his ex-girlfriend Bobbi that he loves her, not his fiancée. The ex finds a microphone cord under a lampshade and demands to know what's really going on. Here's the writer's response:

> I found my voice in my own romantic foibles! I approached *Esquire* and they're interested, so I started taping all these different—but that's not why I came here. It isn't. What I said about seeing you again is true. All my feelings for you. Completely.

The more the writer talks, the worse it sounds:

> I sometimes use the people around me to further my career . . . well, Bobbi, that makes me an American, frankly, and that is about it. Look, I'm not even one of those authors who're out there right now pretending like all their shit is real or, or . . . hiding behind the persona of some twelve-year-old *boy*—I don't do any of that! I am just me and I write amusing stories while changing the names of everybody involved and I don't see who's getting hurt by it.

The writer tears up at this point and says, "I love you . . . not anybody else I've ever known, even this girl I'm supposed to marry . . . no one. Just you."

To show he means business, the writer takes the cassette out of the tape recorder and pulls the tape from its casing. His ex Bobbi walks out of the room, and then the phone rings. It's his fiancée.

"I love you very much," he tells her. "Very, very much . . . and I always will. Yes. I promise. Uh-huh. Will always and always and always . . . *yes,* and always more. *Always.*"

The writer hangs the phone up and winds the tape back into the casing.

When Zella asked me whether our relationship was connected to this book, whether I was going to write about her, I didn't respond (in part, as I said, because the question caught me off-guard). But, as Lance Burton pointed out, when somebody you care about asks you a straight question, you should give them a straight answer. So, Zella, if you're reading this, here's mine: *The two were connected, but not in the way you think—not in the Neil LaBute sort of way. I didn't date you so I could write about you; I dated you because I liked you. And then I wrote about it because it was my job.*

If that distinction makes any sense, please call me.

P.S., I'm still working on this whole trust thing. I've got a long way to go, but now I'm finally moving in the right direction.

Epilogue: One Last Mindfreak

During the course of writing this book I never got to meet Criss Angel. But not for lack of trying. Criss's people turned me down on several occasions. I wrote the bulk of this book in the months that followed the *BeLIEve* premiere, and after those negative reviews came out Angel was understandably reluctant to speak with any journalist.

The day I turned the manuscript for this book over to my editor, I entered a contest to attend the unveiling of the Criss Angel Madame Tussaud wax sculpture. Supposedly Criss was going to be there. Supposedly the contest winner would get a chance to meet him.

I won the contest.

I found an open seat between Luxor president Felix Rappaport and Robin Leach. Angel's whole family was seated before me (I recognized them from *Mindfreak*. Yes, I'm a "loyal"), and so was Carrot Top. Criss walked in the room a minute before the big reveal and made a pretty funny self-deprecating/faux-egotistical joke—something like, "I'm excited to see this sculpture because I'm used to looking at myself in the mirror . . . but now I'll get to see all my perfections in *three* dimensions."

Criss was really nice to me. We talked about Gary Darwin's magic club at Boomers, and I congratulated him on all of his success. I'm pretty sure I meant it. We took a photo with Carrot Top, and then Criss talked with him for a bit.

One evening a couple of months later, I found myself at Las Vegas Athletic Club, on the StairMaster, watching the new season of *Mindfreak*. After a commercial break, a lady who looked vaguely familiar to me appeared on the screen. It was the woman from Madame Tussauds.

Prop comic Scott "Carrot Top" Thompson, me, and Criss Angel. A month after this photo was taken, I single-handedly reunited Thompson with his mentor, rival prop comic Gallagher, after a two-decade feud. But that's a story for another time. . . .

"In just a few moments," the woman said, "we will be unveiling the newest amazing lifelike wax figure of master illusionist Criss Angel."

Cut to Criss: "Thank you so much, ladies and gentlemen. I want to first off thank Madame Tussauds for immortalizing me here in Las Vegas."

Then the camera cut to me. The cameraman must have picked me for the reaction shot, because I was displaying the biggest, dumbest grin in the history of hysterics.

Then back to Criss: "I'm just so thankful and so grateful to Madame Tussauds, and I want to thank all of you for coming today. . . . Well, let's have a look, shall we?"

Then back to me for more grinning.

It's now 2010, and I still work out at Las Vegas Athletic Club. Meaning, I still live in Las Vegas. Initially, I thought I'd be here for a couple of weeks, but the weeks turned into months, and the months turned into years. Like I told my mom, I miscalculated.

I still plan to move back to Chicago, and I still plan to practice personal injury law . . . but I'm not ready yet.

I found a job writing for *Las Vegas Weekly*. I still play low-limit poker a couple nights a week (though I usually do it at Mirage or Wynn because Bellagio won't let me read at the table). I still go clubbing about once a week, only now I get in for free, without waiting in line. I walk to the front of the line and say, "Hi, I'm one of the Nightlife writers for *Las Vegas Weekly*." And I'll be damned if they don't let me in 90 percent of the time.

And I still go to Gary Darwin's magic club at Boomers most Wednesdays.

Have you seen this Elmo Live toy? It's a descendent of Tickle Me Elmo, and I swear it's got twice the charisma of any Vegas performer I've ever seen. Mel, the magician's assistant who introduced me to Oxana, bought one for her son as a Hanukkah gift. When I drove to Mel's house one Wednesday evening to pick her up for Darwin's magic club, I seriously considered kidnapping him. Elmo, not the son.

"If you and Elmo are going to be busy for a while," Mel said, "I'm going to put some moisturizer around my eyes."

"Around your eyes?"

"Burn injury. From back when I was with Criss."

"And Criss is, what, an ex-boyfriend who threw acid on your face?"

"I never told you this? I was Criss Angel's assistant for like three years."

"Uh, *no*, you never told me that."

"Yeah, I did his show in New York, and then the first two seasons of *Mindfreak*."

"You were on *Mindfreak?* You definitely never told me this."

"Remember the metamorphosis episode?"

"Yes . . ."

"Where the girl got burned."

"Yes . . ."

"That was me, with the booty shorts and the Zorro mask, which was latex paint, by the way. What happened was, we were nervous about coverage, so we moved the flames closer to the box. Basically the fire melted the latex to my face. I remember standing on the box, and the flames went up, and I just blacked out. When Criss opened the box and I jumped out, I must have been going on adrenaline because I don't remember any of that. I mean, I've seen the video, so I know it happened, that I got through the trick, but I don't remember it from when it actually happened. It's like I wasn't even controlling my body. Hang on. Let me show you something."

Mel retrieved a shoe box from her bedroom. She opened it up, pulled out the hospital report and a couple photos of her burned face, and handed them to me.

So maybe it wasn't a hoax after all.

"I jumped out of the box and ran backstage, if you remember the episode . . ."

"I remember the episode . . ."

"Yeah, so because I was able to do that, nobody believed I was actually burned or hurt. They thought it was a hoax or something."

"That's awful. Talk about adding insult to injury."

"No kidding."

"It's such a shame," I said.

"What?"

"There's so many untrusting people out there."

Contacting the Author

You can visit me at RickLax.com and reach me at LawyerBoyChicago@gmail.com. If you made it this far, why not drop me an e-mail and let me know what you thought of the book?

Author's Note

British researcher Richard Wiseman carried out a survey with the help of *The Daily Telegraph* in which a majority of respondents admitted to lying about "important" matters every day. Over 60 percent admitted having lied to their partner, and over 80 percent admitted to having lied to secure a job.* Sixty and 80 percent of people *admitted* doing these things. It figures that many people who lied at work or to their partners would have lied about having done so or simply not responded to the survey.†

American researchers have made similar findings.

---

* The respondents justified lying in seeking employment by saying that it was expected of them. David Lieberman, author of *Never Be Lied to Again*, recommends that employers use this expectation to their advantage in weeding out dishonest job applicants (e.g., "As we both know, everybody pads his résumé just a bit. Personally, I think it shows guts. It tells me that the person isn't afraid to take on new responsibilities. Which parts were you most creative with on this résumé?").

† Figuring out what percent of people lie to pollsters is obviously tricky, but the researchers behind the Tucson Garbage Project did just that. The TGP pollsters asked hundreds of people how much beer they consume in one week; then they actually went through the respondents' trash bags and counted the cans. Less than half of those surveyed admitted to drinking any beer, and none of them admitted to drinking eight or more cans per week. The pollsters found beer cans in 76 percent of the trash cans, half of which had eight or more beer cans inside.

Dr. David Knox at East Carolina University found that 92 percent of students admitted to lying to sexual partners.* In *The Day America Told the Truth*, authors James Patterson and Peter Kim reported that 90 percent of Americans polled admitted that they lied about their feelings, their income, their accomplishments, their sex life, or their age.

After receiving his survey results, Wiseman, the British researcher, devised a method to test people's honesty in a more controlled environment. He took over a National Newsagent store and instructed the cashiers to give customers too much change. Customers who paid with a five-pound note received cash for a ten-pound note. Customers who paid with a ten received change for a twenty.

So how many of the customers took the extra cash?

All of them. Many of them walked out of the shop smiling.

Wiseman suspected that some of the customers might have been taking the change because they hadn't noticed they'd been overpaid, so he instructed the cashiers to count the change aloud.

How many customers took the extra cash then?

All of them.

Wiseman next instructed the cashiers to count the money into the subjects' hands and then directly ask

---

* Women lied about being sexually satisfied, and men lied in saying, "I love you."

them the value of the note they had used. According to Wiseman, "Almost no one told the truth. Interestingly, the shoppers often didn't lie straight away but checked that the cashier had no way of knowing which denomination they had used ('Can't you look in the drawer?') before calling the situation in their favor."

In the final phase of the experiment, Wiseman and the other scientists posed as market researchers and asked the customers three questions as they walked out the door:

1. "Do you think journalists are honest?"
2. "Can the Queen be trusted?"
3. "If you were given too much change in a shop, would you own up and return the money?"

The customers answered the first two questions decisively ("no," "yes"), but did everything they could to avoid answering the third (e.g., "I don't usually look at my change," "I never really check my change").

The point is, virtually everybody lies when the opportunity presents itself.

Accordingly, I'm not telling you to believe that the stories you read in this book are true because "I never lie" or because "it's not in my nature to be deceptive." We all lie, and it's in our nature to be deceptive. I'm telling you that the stories in this book are true because *as it happens, I told them truthfully.*

Now, that said, some of the people described in this book are composites based on the people I met in Las Vegas. I reconstructed dialogues by memory and altered details of certain events (e.g., the times and places at which those incidents occurred). Accordingly, this book is not 100 percent accurate. I'd put it in the high nineties.

Acknowledgments and Plugs

Thanks to the security guard who helped move Elena's body from the cab to the bench. You really went above and beyond the call of duty that night, and however much you're getting paid isn't enough. Thanks to the ambulance drivers and to the Chicago Police Department officers who helped out with "the Elena situation."

Thanks to my mom for moving me from Detroit to Las Vegas. Turns out it's a really long drive. Who knew? Also, thanks for loaning me your car for those few weeks—the ones that turned into years. Thanks to my dad for bringing me to Las Vegas as a kid, year after year, and for not freaking out when, immediately after law school, I said I was heading there to hang out with magicians. Thanks also for becoming my de facto *Lawyer Boy* publicist.

Thanks to the whole gang at Gary Darwin's magic club for welcoming me, teaching me, and making me feel like "the normal one" for a change. Thanks to AJ and Jeremy and Craig at StreetOfCards.TV. If you want to check out Gary Darwin's magic club but don't live in

Las Vegas, head to StreetOfCards.TV Wednesday night at 10:00 P.M. Pacific Time and you can see a live broadcast. You can also join the chat room and make fun of me in real time, like everybody else on StreetOfCards .TV. . . .

Thanks to Kyle & Mistie (KnightMagic.com), and to Bizzaro (SmappDooda.com). Thanks also to Chris Smith, who makes some of the cleverest magic tricks money can buy. If you've got some extra spending cash and you want to blow your friends away, head to Magic Smith.com and buy a couple of Mr. Smith's illusions. Thanks to Bram at EveryMagician.com. If you live in Las Vegas and want to book a magician for a gig, Bram's the guy to talk to. Thanks to Jason, and to Scott, and to Shedini, and to Melanie, and to all the guys I see each week whose names I can never quite remember. And thanks to Gary.

Thanks to *MAGIC* editor Stan Allen for lunch, for the stories, and for putting out a great magazine (MagicMagazine.com). If you're interested in learning more about magic, treat yourself to a subscription to *MAGIC*. When I was eleven or twelve, I got in trouble this one day at Camp Nebagamon, and my counselor punished me by taking away my stack of *MAGIC* magazines. It just killed me. Point is, the magazine is great.

Thanks to Stan's buddy Lance Burton for his time and for his generosity (LanceBurton.com). If you want to see dove magic done right, fly to Las Vegas and watch Lance do it. Thanks to Wayne for setting me up with tickets to Lance's show and for setting up our interview. Thanks also to Keith Barry (KeithBarry.com) for his time, for lunch, and for the awesome coin trick. I have no idea how you did it, sir. The guys at Gary Darwin's magic club had some theories, but I wasn't satisfied with any of them. You fooled me good.

Last on the magic front, thanks to Joshua Jay and Gabe Fajuri.

Thanks to Artisan the PUA for showing me how it's done. Yes, a lot of PUAs are cheesy and creepy . . . but not Artisan. He's the real deal. If you want to book an appointment with the guy and see for yourself, you can find him at TheAttractiveMan.com.

Thanks to Professors Michael Borer, Sally Caldwell, and Charles Ford for their professional insight. The way things worked out, I didn't get to include my interview with Dr. Ford in the final draft of this book, but if you'd like to hear some real deception insight, pick up a copy of Dr. Ford's book *Lies! Lies!! Lies!!!: The Psychology of Deceit.*

Thanks to Rusty Slusser for the amazing mask. If you need to disguise yourself for whatever (legal) reason, head to SpfxMasks.com and pick up one of his creations. I've scoured the Internet and have come to the conclusion that SPFX masks are in a class of their own. Also, thanks to Dave Brecher and to Harish Mandyam for making the mask storyline possible.

Thanks to card counter Jeff Ma for his time and for the stories (CitizenSportsInc.com). Thanks to poker pro Mike Caro (and Diane) for the lovely lunch and for the books and DVDs. If you've got a great bad-beat story, I'm sure Mike would want to hear it, so head to Poker1 .com, find Mike's contact info, and type away. (And while you're there, you should check out his books and DVDs. My favorite is *Caro's Most Profitable Hold'em Advice: The Complete Missing Arsenal*, but *Caro's Book of Poker Tells: The Psychology and Body Language of Poker* is a classic.) Also, while we're on the topic of poker, thanks to Julie and Jessica and the rest of the gang at the Mirage poker room for letting me read at the table. Thanks also to the fine people at the Wynn.

Thanks to Dean and the gang at the Town Square Borders—you guys run the prettiest, cleanest bookstore I've ever seen.

Thanks to Bryan, Bruce, and everybody else at *Las Vegas Weekly* and Greenspun Media for giving me an excuse to hang out in Las Vegas longer than originally planned. Thanks to my talented editors, Ken and Spencer. Big thanks to Joe Brown for the support and for the careful edits (on this book). More big thanks to *Las Vegas Weekly* editor in chief Scott Dickensheets, a man whose work product proves there *is* such a thing as a free lunch, after all. If you don't believe me, pick up a (free) copy of *Las Vegas Weekly* (or head to LasVegasWeekly.com) and see for yourself.

Thanks to Beth and Mo for their hospitality, to Natalie for the adventures, to Brittany for keeping me on task at Borders, to Kimberly for the excitement, to Stella, Cindi, Rachel, Sharon, and Josh for the literary camaraderie. Thanks to Sylvia for the support, consistency, warmth, and fun.

Thanks to my awesome agent, Ted Weinstein (tw literary.com), who tells it like it is, and to my acquiring editor, David Moldawer, who made this book possible. For a lively discussion of science, technology, and pop culture, visit David at Podcast.Moldawer.com.

Thanks to my current editor, Matt Martz, for pushing through 2009 with me. I truly feel that we made a kick-ass book together.

Above all, thanks to "Oxana" for being the number one best roommate in the history of confined space. Thanks for allowing me into your life, for bringing me along on so many of your adventures, and for participating in so many of mine.

Remember the photo in Oxana's bathroom—the one of her and Inessa naked? Well, the frame that holds it up has this quote on its bottom that goes: "We didn't ask for this life." I don't know what it means, but I know it feels right.